SHADOWED

HOW I BECAME THE
SEX-TRAFFICKED MOTHER
NEXT DOOR

JULIE WHITEHEAD

HOUNDSTOOTH
PRESS

SHADOWED
How I Became the Sex-Trafficked Mother Next Door
First Edition

ISBN 978-1-5445-4034-4 *Hardcover*
      978-1-5445-4033-7 *Paperback*
      978-1-5445-4032-0 *Ebook*

To my incredible husband whom I adore.
Thank you for saving me in every way a person can be saved.

To my children who are fighters.
I love you more than words can say.

To all the victims and survivors out there:
may you find the hope and the strength to heal.

CONTENTS

ACKNOWLEDGMENTS

This book wouldn't have been written if it weren't for my amazing husband Barry. Thank you for reading endless copies and for all the support that was necessary for me to even attempt this. I am so in love with you, and you are my very best friend! Thank you to Sam and Kacie Malouf, without whom I would never have believed in myself enough to tell my story. Thank you to Schae Richards for guiding me on this journey, around all the twists and turns! Thank you to Aniko Mahan and Jake Neeley for directing this whole process and for your unwavering support. Thank you to Beth Thompson and Alison Hart for your input and advice. Thank you, Dr. Vuckovic, Dr. Wagner, and Shannon Haley for keeping me from falling to pieces and supporting me along the way. Thank you to Randy Garn for sharing all your insights and wisdom and for your support. Thank you, Michael Levin for your amazing contribution and your incredible talent! Thank you, Elizabeth Smart for writing the foreword.

You are an inspiration to so many people and I am very honored to know you. Thank you to my new friends at Scribe Media for all you've done to help make this book a reality. Thank you to everyone who has had an influence in this book being written. Thank you to the Malouf Foundation, whose people are amazing and have renewed my hope in the human race. Thank you for all you do for victims and survivors and for changing the world and making it a better place.

FOREWORD

The first time I met Julie, she was speaking at the Malouf Foundation Summit on a panel with other survivors of sexual violence. I could tell that she was facing her fears in real time when the moderator of the panel asked if Julie would like to share her story. She took a deep breath, collected herself, and spoke.

As I listened to the horrific cycle of abuse she endured, I was struck by her resilience. Her voice was quiet, but she was composed and self-assured as she shared the darkest parts of her life.

Since I first saw her speak, my foundation, the Elizabeth Smart Foundation, joined forces with the Malouf Foundation. Julie and I both serve on the Malouf Foundation Survivor Advisory Board, where we work together on advocacy and awareness. She is particularly involved with the OnWatch program, which is a free online resource led by survivors who share their stories to educate on the signs of human trafficking.

Julie has said she has always wanted to write a book, even as a little girl. Her experiences were the last thing she would choose to write about, but what she felt she was supposed to write about. Writing a book about your trauma can be overwhelming, but Julie and I both found new perspectives on our stories through the process.

I hope reading Julie's story gives you a new perspective, as well. It's easy to look at someone else's life and make judgments. You can ask me, "Why didn't you run?" Or like the judge in Julie's case, you can question why she didn't scream out for help when her trafficker took her into public places. We recognize these questions come from a genuine desire to understand, but they are rooted in a complete lack of perspective. It's much more difficult to step into someone else's pain and fear and understand why they made the choices they did.

Every choice Julie made was for survival. For herself, and her children.

Julie endured as a series of predators exploited her vulnerabilities for thirty-one years. She fought for her life. Not in the way we often hear the phrase "fighting for our lives"—how many people think survivors should physically fight, verbally fight, or actively attack. Julie faced sustained and continuous survival in a life many would find unlivable.

And today, she willingly embraces vulnerability to share her story and protect others from sexual exploitation. That takes deep, deep wells of resilience and compassion.

Julie and I recently had a conversation about her life today on my podcast. She recognized her beautiful family, loving relationships, and healing—which will be a part of her life forever. Writing this book was part of her healing journey, and she believes that if she can only help one person, the pain of disclosure is worth it.

I hope we can all learn from Julie. She describes a system that failed her and a family who denied her healing, yet she approaches life with compassion and grace for others. We can create communities that lift up and believe in incredible survivors—if we listen to more people like Julie!

—Elizabeth Smart
Kidnapping Survivor and Founder of
the Elizabeth Smart Foundation

October 14, 2022

SEX TRAFFICKING IS AN AMERICAN STORY TOO

It's Friday afternoon and you're casually chatting with some of the other moms outside your kids' preschool, comparing notes on what all of you will be doing this weekend. Backyard barbecues, swimming, maybe a movie, right?

But then you notice that one of the moms isn't saying much. In fact, come to think of it, she *never* talks about what she's going to do over the weekend.

That's because you couldn't imagine in a million years where she'll be and how she'll pass the time.

That mom, whom you might also know from church or simply from seeing her in the supermarket, at PTA meetings, or around town, won't be going to the beach or to the movies.

Instead, she will be trafficked for sex against her will.

She will be driven to a truck stop, to a motel in a distant state, or even across the US–Mexico border, where she will be forced to have sex with strangers. She may be drugged, she risks being beaten, she will be videoed in the act, and if she dares to tell a soul, her trafficker has threatened to tell everyone in her innocent suburban community that she is a prostitute.

If your kids and my kids were in the same preschool, when Friday afternoon came along, I would be the mom not telling you or the other moms what my weekend plans were.

That's because I was trafficked.

For nearly half a year, I went through the most horrific of ordeals while living a double life. During the week, I was a regular mom. On the weekends, men could buy me and do with me as they saw fit.

I could have been killed, either by my captor or by any of the men who paid to have sex with me.

I felt so invisible. There I was, being sold for sex, and it felt as if nobody in my own community even noticed.

How did this happen? you might ask.

Long story short, I was in a brutal, abusive marriage, and the nice, friendly man in my community who helped me break free of that marriage took advantage of me and put me to work essentially as a sex slave.

This may sound crazy or impossible but let me assure you—it's the absolute truth.

I wouldn't say I've ever had it easy. I grew up with a sexually abusive father, married an abusive and violent husband,

and then had to live through my experiences in sex trafficking. Despite all that, I can assure you that I'm one of the lucky ones. That's because I got out of trafficking...alive.

In these pages, I'm going to share with you every detail of what I had to endure as a woman trafficked for sex while maintaining the charade that I was just your typical girl next door with some little kids and a marriage that hadn't quite worked out.

I'm telling my story because too many women have found themselves in the same position: trafficked for sex, in constant fear of being murdered, and believing that there is no way out.

When we think of sex trafficking, to the extent that we think about it at all, it doesn't feel like an American phenomenon. This couldn't happen here, could it? Isn't it just something that happens in unfortunate countries where the economic standards are lower, corruption flourishes, and laws against sex trafficking aren't rigorously enforced?

I'm here to tell you that it happens right here. I'm hardly the first woman to endure sex trafficking, but, again, I am one of the lucky ones in that I found a way out.

If you are going through the same thing that I went through, my purpose is to give you the courage to make your own escape.

If you are a legislator or a social services worker or a journalist, I want you to know my story in depth because my story is all too common. I want to empower you with the facts so that you can make a difference for other women, children, and men.

Sex trafficking isn't something that only happens a world away. It's happening in your community, in your neighborhood, and it might involve one of the other mothers in your child's preschool.

It might even be you.

This is my story; this is an American story; this is our story. And it's time that our story was told.

SHADOWED

ONE

THE FINAL TRIP

My last trip with Eric was to Hailey, Idaho, a quiet mountain town a few hours outside of Boise.

Trips. This was his word, not mine, a total euphemism. What we were doing was anything but a vacation.

Eric wanted to leave that night, on short notice. We had been going out almost every weekend for the last three or four months, starting in November; it was February already, so it didn't catch me totally off guard.

There was no need to scramble to find a place for my kids, as I had already lost custody of them, which made planning easier. I used to drop them at my parents' house whenever Eric wanted to go out on a trip. I was estranged from my parents after separating from my husband, Richard, so we hardly talked, but they wanted to maintain a relationship with their grandkids. My father had been abusive when I was little, and so was Richard, so I hadn't really wanted my kids around any of them, but it was better than having them around Eric.

Eric was a long-haul trucker, and he used his semitrailer rig for these trips. It was my job to ready the truck before we left. I cleared trash off the floorboards and dash. If he was going to haul cargo along the way, it was sometimes my job to do the loading. I picked up snacks for the road, though these were for him, not me.

Eric always made me do all the physical labor, even though I was a tiny woman. He had once taken me out to Montana during a snowstorm. I came back from using a gas station restroom, something that was often not even allowed, to find him putting snow chains on the tires. He had me stand out in the cold to help him, even though he had me in skimpy clothes. When we later got stuck in the snow, he gave me the shovel and just watched as I dug the tires out.

Packing my own stuff before these trips was quick and easy, as I wasn't allowed to bring anything more than toiletries, a change of clothes, and some extra underwear. No need to worry about outfits: Eric picked out my clothes, usually short skirts or daisy dukes, halter tops, that sort of thing, skimpy outfits way too tight for a grown woman. He had me wearing things from the girls' department even though I was in my early thirties. Kids' clothes fold up small and fit easily into a backpack.

Clothes were a privilege, not a right, when we went out together. He sometimes had me strip down to nothing before getting into the back of the sleeper cab. This made me feel vulnerable and trapped, as I couldn't slip off unseen as a naked woman at the truck stop, and it would be dangerous and humiliating to even try. So he usually kept me in the back of the cab with the curtain drawn; no one even knew I was there.

This time, on our trip out to Hailey, he had me in shorts and a tank top, which was completely inappropriate given the temperature up north in February. At least it was clothing and allowed me a shred of dignity. I was still cold, though, especially when the truck had stopped, so I huddled in the back with a blanket over me—when he let me use it.

Abuse like this, which I had been dealing with in one form or another my whole life, had taught me how to disassociate and leave my own body, leave my own mind. I lay in the back of the cab with the curtains drawn and tried to just turn my brain off.

The diesel engine rumbled, rattling the whole rig, and I could feel the highway beneath us. The hiss of the cold wind whipped past as we drove. The whole world was out there, and I was stuck in here, so I tried my best not to be present for any of it. He could own my body, but not my mind. That's what I liked to think, anyway, and it would take me years of learning about trauma to see otherwise.

LOST IN PLAIN SIGHT

At the time, I didn't know we were headed to Hailey, or even Idaho for that matter. Eric never told me where we were going ahead of time. This was something I always had to piece together on my own along the way. Figuring out my general location gave me a sense of comfort, some small sense of agency in a situation where I had almost none.

I was usually in the back with the curtain drawn when he was driving, so I couldn't see street signs. However, I could tell from the stops and turns which route we were taking out of town. Gas stations and truck stops provided a variety of clues. When we stopped for the restroom, I would scan store shelves for postcards, travel brochures, state shot glasses, anything that would give away the location. Montana, California, Idaho, Nevada: the outlines of the states were easy to spot. Gas station receipts discarded in the parking lot or left hanging from the fuel pump had full addresses printed at the top. Both landscape and landscaping might provide clues. Palm trees usually meant California; brush might mean high desert somewhere, maybe Utah, maybe Nevada.

Sometimes, I would actually recognize my location. We were coming back from a trip to California once and pulled over at the exit leading to my grandparents' house. They had recently moved away, and there was no way I would have been able to run and make it to the house anyway, but it was still a comfort knowing where we were, though it was also disorienting. What was happening to me seemed so unreal and separate from my real life back home with the kids that it was jarring to have the real world and this new reality intersect.

Hailey was also a place I recognized. Eric pulled over and opened the curtain to let me up into the passenger seat, even though I usually only rode in the back. Maybe he was bored or lonely, or maybe he wanted someone to be nasty to. I don't know why, but he let me up front. I recognized local landmarks flying by out the window from when my parents took us on vacations at a nearby lake when we were kids. We would stay at a lodge, watch live music, and go down to the water to go tubing and catch minnows.

This place gave me no nostalgia, as I had not had a happy childhood either, but the present moment was too horrific and terrifying to linger on the past anyway. Still, I was glad to have located myself here in Hailey. *Hailey,* I told myself. *Hailey, Idaho.* Just naming where we were calmed me down a little.

This wasn't purely psychological. There was good reason to want to know my location—I was absolutely terrified of Eric leaving me behind somewhere. I would have no way to get home, nothing on me, maybe not even clothes on my back, with no clue where I was or how to get back home. What if he had taken me over a border? He had before. How would I get back home with no money and no papers, unable to even speak the local language?

My horror at being left stranded had the curious effect of making me reliant on my captor. As awful as Eric was, I needed him to protect me and get me home. Forget trying to escape; I was terrified of being left behind.

Although I didn't always know *where* I was, I knew full well *why* we were going. The anticipation was always terrible.

When we got to Hailey, we stopped at a small warehouse. Eric backed the trailer up to the building. He had had me load several big white cargo boxes into the trailer before we headed out. I had no idea what was in them. Maybe guns, maybe drugs—not everything he hauled was legal.

Eric put the truck in park and killed the engine before climbing down from the cab and taking me inside. Though cold and dark, the warehouse offered some shelter from the elements outside.

Eric pointed at a metal stool in the corner and told me to take a seat. "Don't move," he warned, as if I needed warning.

Eric went to the office in the back and knocked on the door until someone let him in. I sat there alone in the dark, waiting for him to come back but also dreading his return. The warehouse wasn't heated, and I was not dressed for the occasion. My whole body was shaking, and I could feel the cold radiating up from the metal stool and through my shorts, but I dared not move from the spot. I huddled up and rubbed my exposed arms and shoulders and waited, just as I was told.

Voices floated over from the office, but I couldn't make out individual words as they echoed through the warehouse. I assumed Eric was working out some deal, but were they negotiating the content of the cargo boxes or was I the cargo?

Often, it was me. That was the whole point of these "trips." Though I didn't have the words for it at the time, Eric was a human trafficker, and I was being trafficked. He might have also had some other legitimate business to conduct, but I knew he was always moving at least some contraband—because it was me.

COCKROACHES

This had been going on for months now. Almost every weekend it was the same, with him dressing me up—if I was lucky enough to have clothes at all—and taking me out on the road in his semitruck. We went all over the country, even over the border to Mexico, where he would sell my body to strangers. Sometimes he would just give me away without any financial payoff, out of the sheer cruelty and deranged pleasure he felt watching others rape me.

We went to brothels, casinos, abandoned warehouses, condemned houses, seedy motels, and occasionally even nice hotels. There were sometimes a line of men waiting their turn, either for me or some other woman or girl.

At times, he would just take me to truck stops—hotbeds for prostitution and trafficking—and start soliciting interested truckers. He would use the CB radio or the second phone he kept "for business," tucked away in a maroon duffel bag full of guns, knives, and drugs, and a whole assortment of pills and powders. I wasn't supposed to touch the bag; I wasn't even supposed to look when it came out. He told me to avert my eyes, but I would peek, and he let me, as he wanted me to know he was armed. Everything was a constant push-pull between him wanting to keep me in the dark while also making it clear how much danger I was in.

Eric was from Peru and spoke better Spanish than English; most of the men he brought me to were also Hispanic, usually other truck drivers. They spoke in Spanish, and the language barrier helped keep me in the dark about what was going on. There was no way for me to know what he was saying over the CB radio. I could only pick out a few words here and there, usually just my name. *Julie*. Or one of his creepy pet names for me, like *Little Miss Sunshine*. Everything else was incomprehensible.

It never took Eric long to find interested men at the truck stop, if he even had to get on the CB radio at all. On one of our first trips, driving up north toward Idaho, we pulled into a busy truck stop during a windstorm, with the wind blasting so hard that all the big rigs had to pull over because it wasn't safe on the highway.

"You're going to want a pill in you for this," he said, reaching for the drugs he often fed me.

Knowing what this was code for, that he planned to sell my body, I took the drugs happily, hoping to zonk myself out. I used to refuse them. Not anymore.

The place was so packed that the trucks were all lined up inches apart, packed in together like sardines, so close it was hard to know how they had even gotten them in together that way.

"There are cockroaches here," Eric said, which was his word for prostitutes.

The prostitutes would walk down the line and knock on the door of each truck until someone cracked the door, he said, which was how you gave permission for them to come up. We hadn't been there but a minute before a knock came at the door. Eric reached over and turned the handle. The door opened, and outside was a man standing with a woman who looked totally out of it, maybe drugged or maybe just really high; it was hard to say. She seemed a few years older than me. They had her dressed up in skimpy clothing too. I felt an obvious and immediate kinship in that we were clearly in a similar situation.

Eric and the man exchanged words in Spanish, and then the man helped the woman up into the cab. She looked into the back of the truck and made eye contact with me, which Eric didn't like, so he reached back, shoved me down, and pulled the curtain closed. I could still see through the gap in the curtain, though, and a terrible foreboding overcame me. I just couldn't look away. I watched as Eric suddenly smacked the woman in the head and sent her reeling backward out of the truck.

Her body hit the concrete with a loud thud, and I was afraid she was dead. The man who had brought her over just laughed about it and helped her back up into the passenger seat.

"I'll handle this," Eric said to the man. "Get her out of here."

Eric then told me to get out, so I had to climb over this unconscious, possibly dead woman to exit the cab.

The man outside led me over to the truck stop, where a worker stood at the counter. I was drugged and tripping over myself the whole way.

Inside the truck stop, the man at the counter took one look at me and shook his head no. "We don't want that in here."

The man I was with just ignored him and took me back into the showers, leading me by the hand. The man at the counter didn't try to stop us—no one ever tried to stop what was happening. You could see they knew what this was, that I was obviously drugged, but even when they spoke up like this, they never actually did anything. No one kicked us out; no one called the police. They just let it happen, not wanting to get involved.

There was another man waiting in the showers to have his way with me, and I was handed off to him. There was a whole line of men waiting, apparently, and they just kept coming in one after the other. The whole ordeal was horrific, but I just turned my face away and blocked it out as best I could, as I had learned to do a thousand times before.

But what I couldn't shake was the image of that woman, half conscious, in Eric's truck. I hoped she was okay.

When the man took me back to Eric's truck, there was blood on the steering wheel and Eric's hands, but the woman was gone. It was only when I climbed back into the back of the cab that I saw her there, wrapped up tight in a patchwork quilt, her hair poking out the top. Though I wanted to check on her, I just couldn't bring myself to even touch her. I was afraid she was already dead.

Before we could leave, Eric said she had to go. The other man helped him lift her out of the truck and carry her away, one holding her under the arms and the other one getting the legs, so that she really looked like a corpse. When Eric came back five minutes later, the man was gone, and he didn't mention her again.

This was all terrifying, of course, as it underscored the mortal danger I was in. Eric wasn't making hollow threats. He actually could just kill me, as he was clearly capable of murder.

I always felt guilty when there were other women since I couldn't do anything to help them. Another time, Eric had taken me to a warehouse in the middle of a barren, rocky field. He sat me down outside in a folding chair and told me not to move, not even to turn my head. I sat there, just kicking rocks to pass the time. As the hours slipped away, I couldn't help but peek when I heard cars and trucks pulling up, along with several big black vans, so I knew there were other people there.

Eric eventually led me inside the warehouse, where a group of men surrounded a blonde woman about my age, maybe a little younger, completely naked, zip-tied to a metal cot. She wasn't making much noise but was struggling to free herself to no avail. She too caught my eye, looking desperate for help, but there was nothing I could do. These men terrified me, so I leaned in close to Eric for fear they would do the same to me, as if he were my protector, not the person who had brought me here. You could see the fear in her eyes. It was too much, and I had to look away.

Later, Eric took me back outside and returned me to my chair. I waited a few more hours before he collected me and took me away.

To this day, I suffer from terrible survivor's guilt for not having helped that woman, any of these women, but what could I have done for any of them? Nothing but risk getting us all killed. Still, the guilt follows you forever.

DRUGGED

Those terrible months are a blur now, a hazy nightmare of being forced to do things against my will, over and over. Eric often had me seeing five, ten men a night, sometimes more, just one after another. This was excruciatingly painful and pushed my body and soul to the breaking point.

My most basic needs went unmet. I was always starving, always thirsty and dehydrated. Eric rarely took me into restaurants with him to get food. He might toss me leftovers or a water bottle here and there, but not until my mouth was so dry that it hurt to swallow and my stomach was eating itself. I couldn't even go to the bathroom without permission. Sometimes my bladder felt ready to rupture. He didn't care, wouldn't pull over, and when he did, he often made me urinate on the side of the highway with cars zipping by.

I had terrible migraines constantly, my head always throbbing, but I dared not complain no matter how much my vision faltered or my stomach turned. Eric had proved his viciousness enough times to keep me silent. He was always blasting Hispanic music in the truck. If I made the mistake of asking him to turn it down because my head hurt, he would just crank it louder. At this point, I knew better than to complain.

The only thing that helped dull the pain were the drugs he fed me. At first, I didn't want to take them, as they made everything feel more surreal and nightmarish, but refusal wasn't an option, and eventually I came to appreciate how they numbed me or even made me black out.

My memories are sketchy and fragmented, with the nights blurring into one another. Even now, they're just flashes of images from the unceasing nightmare that was my life: the busted neon signs over seedy motels, the glare of interstate high-mast lighting bearing down on the tops of semitrucks, the averted gaze of truck stop attendants, men leading me from one truck to another, the water-stained ceilings of cheap motel rooms. It's all a blur, even the men. I rarely saw the same one twice. Though they came in different shapes, sizes, ethnicities, and backgrounds, they were effectively one indistinguishable, amorphous blob of terrible men.

I had no idea what Eric was actually giving me. Much later, I found out he was feeding me Rohypnol, better known as the date rape drug. There were other drugs too, sometimes a cocktail of pills. There was one pill he called Mexican Valium. To this day, I still have no idea what was in those pills, but they did the trick, always knocking me out hard. After taking one, I couldn't stand or walk on my own. The pill would eventually cause me to black out entirely so that I could only remember the before and after of a night, not the sordid details, which was a cruel blessing. Rohypnol left me foggy but basically still lucid. My vision would get hazy, my mind fuzzy, the air almost liquid as the world turned soft, but I was still basically present. The harder drugs, the Mexican Valium, could make whole hours just disappear. I preferred those, in a way, even if it was scary not knowing what had happened to me while I was out. It was better not to know.

The drugs made me so woozy and weak in the knees that it was hard to move. In hotel rooms or brothels, I would just lie in bed lifeless while the men did their thing. Truck stops were another matter. I had to get around from one truck to another, which was impossible on my own. The men would have to help me down from Eric's semitruck and over to their own because I couldn't stand up straight without their help. I literally had to lean on my own rapists for support.

Being sober was often worse. Eric once took me over the Nevada border to go to the casinos in Wendover, which were popular with Utahns who couldn't gamble at home due to the influence of the church. The woman driving the car was his sister, and I suspected the other woman was too. I was stone-cold sober while he had me follow him around the casinos. I had to keep my hand on his shoulder while he moved between the different slot machines. He had me all dressed up in this tacky, shimmery dress that was supposed to be sexy, so I knew what was coming later.

When he told me it was "time" and gave me a laced, funny-tasting drink, I was actually relieved not to be sober for what was going to come next. His sisters had already peeled off and were doing their own thing, so Eric walked me to the attached hotel and to a room. He knocked twice, and the door creaked open.

Eric took me inside, got me in bed, and took all my clothes off; then a shirtless man stepped out of the bathroom, still wearing a cowboy hat. He also had a giant, western-style belt buckle holding up his pants. Not wanting to see his face, I just trained my eyes on that buckle and followed it across the room.

Everything is fuzzy after that, but Eric left me there at some point while men came in and out of the room. I have the drugs to thank for not remembering much of it. The last thing

I remember was just lying there afterward, looking at the big casino lights outside in the parking lot.

When Eric collected me later, he and his sisters were all trashed and wanted me to drive us home. I wasn't in any shape to drive either, still coming down off the drugs, but Eric said I was better off than they were. We nearly died on the way home when I almost crashed into a cement barrier coming off the freeway. I couldn't believe how cheap life was to them—even their own lives, it seemed.

NO ESCAPE

Escape from this nightmare seemed impossible, though people who haven't lived through this kind of abuse will find it hard to understand. They wonder why you don't just try to escape.

In fact, I *did* try to escape several times. Eric quickly showed me that it wasn't worth the risk.

He once took me to a restaurant in Mexico, actually bringing me inside to eat at a table, which rarely happened. Seeing all the patrons going about their lives and happily sharing a meal made me feel particularly indignant, and when Eric made some cruel comment, I just snapped and threw my whole plate of food right into his lap. His eyes lit on fire with rage, and I took off running but didn't get far before he caught me and dragged me back to the truck.

Another time, we were plowing through a blizzard near Island Park, Idaho, a little mountain town, which I recognized because my parents used to take us camping there when we were little. Visibility was near zero, and I was terrified of going over the side of a cliff. Eric couldn't see the white lines marking the lane and called me up to spot them for him, but it was impossible to see anything with all the snow coming down. Eric got mad and started screaming about how I was a terrible person, a horrible mother, somehow both a whore and a boring prude at once. He started shoving me hard against the door, over and over. My head was just banging off the door, rattling me to the core.

Eventually, not able to take the abuse anymore, I reached for the handle and opened the door. Without thinking, I jumped from the moving semi. We were going slowly enough in the blizzard that the snow was able to break my fall. Completely uninjured, I jumped up and bolted into the woods.

There were cabins in the woods not far from there, so I headed in that direction, or what I thought was that direction. I was a little turned around, not entirely sure which way the town was. If I could find it, maybe I could call the police. I didn't know, wasn't thinking, and was just trying to get away. I was acting almost purely on instinct. Unfortunately, the snow was much too deep for me to make any headway. My feet sank with each step. I wasn't dressed for the cold, still wearing the dainty clothes Eric had me in. Not wanting to get stuck or lost and freeze to death, I turned back toward the main road and headed farther down, away from Eric and the truck.

When a car started coming down the road, I jumped up and down and waved my arms frantically to flag its occupants. They started to slow just as Eric caught up to me and tackled me to the ground. The people in the car hesitated when Eric took me by the hair and started dragging me back to the truck. The car sped up and took off, disappearing around the bend. As usual, people just don't want to get involved.

Eric sometimes forced me to relieve myself along the side of the road. One time I needed to go, and he wouldn't stop. I kept calling from the back of the cab, telling him I was about to burst. He finally pulled over at an exit but just parked on the triangle between the highway and the off-ramp. He pulled me down from the cab and wanted me to do it right there by the truck with traffic flying by on both sides.

This wasn't the first time he had done this sort of thing, but I wasn't having it that day. There was a Home Depot off the exit, so I took off running in that direction. I ran along the exit ramp and nearly tripped and tumbled down the grassy embankment trying to get away. Eric was pursuing on foot, but I had a good lead and made it to the parking lot. I weaved between cars trying to lose him and then made my way into the store.

There wasn't anyone at the front of the store, so I ducked into the restroom to hide. This was a mistake, I realized instantaneously. I was now trapped. I locked the door and hid in a stall.

Eric caught up and started banging on the door. I waited and waited, hoping security would make him leave, but eventually I lost my nerve. I was afraid he was going to knock the door down and kill me on the spot. Fearing his wrath, I came out and let him take me back to the truck.

Another time, he was screaming at me while we were driving through Ogden, a town outside Salt Lake City, when I decided to bolt. Although he was always screaming about something, this time I had had enough. While we were stopped at a red light, I jumped from the truck and took off running down the road in the opposite direction.

Eric immediately flipped the truck around in the middle of the intersection. Horns were honking like wild. He didn't care. He was coming up behind me quickly, so I cut across several lanes of traffic and headed in the other direction. This time it took him longer to flip around, which gave me time to slip inside an auto parts store.

I came running through the front door looking like a wild woman. One of the clerks looked concerned. "Are you okay?"

"No, I'm not," I said.

The door at the front of the store dinged. There was Eric, coming up the aisle toward me. I clammed up at the sight of him.

"Is everything okay?" the clerk asked again.

Eric came up from behind and wrapped his hand around the back of my neck, squeezing hard. It was not a friendly or gentle gesture.

Now the clerk really looked concerned. "Is everything okay here?"

"Yeah, we're fine," Eric said. He walked me out, still holding me by the back of my neck.

Each of these times, Eric would drag me back to the truck and punish me immediately. He would undo his belt and start whipping me or just rape me right there on the spot.

This wasn't just punishment, but a reminder of what he could do to me whenever he wanted. He made sure I lived in fear at all times. This is why he made sure I caught sight of the guns he was always toting around.

I once considered reaching for a gun casually lying out on the bed while someone was raping me, but what would I do if it wasn't loaded, or I missed, or I couldn't work the safety right? They might well kill me, or they might punish me in ways that would make me *wish* I were dead. Eric knew all my greatest fears and weaknesses. He had taken countless pictures of me with other men and threatened repeatedly to send them to my ex-husband so that I would lose my kids. Then, when he did send them and I did lose my kids, he threatened to send more so that I would never get them back.

So I learned not to fight back, not to resist, not to run. I had to survive, if not for myself, then for my kids.

But compliance wasn't enough to avoid Eric's wrath. He would find fault with me no matter how well I behaved. He often accused me of "cheating" on him with the men he let rape me.

"You'll do it with anybody," he said.

This was distorted beyond belief, but you couldn't argue with him, as it only made things worse. He was just trying to gaslight me, make me feel insane, so there was no point in arguing. Every moment was slow-motion torture, whether he was actively raping me, beating me, or just playing mind games.

He was always playing mind games to keep me feeling trapped. He would do anything to keep me tied to him. He even told me he wanted to get me pregnant. The reason was clear. Having a child together would be the ultimate leverage over me, a way to keep me tied to him forever.

"I am not having a baby with you," I told him flatly.

"Yes, you are," he shouted.

"No," I said again.

He reached over me to unlatch the passenger door and shoved me backward. I went flying out of the cab and landed hard on the asphalt.

We were at a roadside Mexican market in Ogden, outside a fruit stand. A crowd of shoppers circled around to make sure I was okay. Somehow, I had managed not to hit my head, which was fortunate because a fall from that height could easily have cracked my skull open.

Eric started shouting at the people trying to help me up, chasing them off. I don't know what he was saying, but it must have been threatening because everyone dispersed quickly. They watched, doing nothing, as he pulled me back up into the truck and pulled away—further proof that as concerned as people might be, no one ever wants to get involved in a dangerous or bad situation.

He was constantly devising inventive new ways to humiliate and dehumanize me. He would sometimes lie on top of me in the sweltering heat of the cab, all of his clothes off and his belly over my mouth so I couldn't breathe. When I was frantic for air and fighting back, he would allow me just a gasp before smothering me again. Sometimes he would bring me up in the front of the cab without my clothes on, where other cars could see, even forcing me to perform oral sex on him while he drove. He would make me flash other truckers, ordering me to press my naked body up against the windows at his command. Some would slow down and sound their horns as we pulled up to them.

Eric got off on this kind of cruelty. He enjoyed it in the same way he enjoyed raping me. Like all the men he foisted on me, Eric wasn't raping me for sex. He was raping to rape. The sadism coupled with the victim's extreme helplessness were integral to the act. They got off on your fear and humiliation and power-lessness and suffering.

The other reason not to resist was that, as bad as things were, they could always get worse. Eric made sure I was always aware of this fact. He once showed me a homemade pornographic video of a girl tied to a cot while men carved up her flesh. The girl zip-tied to the cot in the warehouse had reminded me of this video. I couldn't get her or that video out of my head. I don't know if that's what they did to her, but I knew I didn't want them to do it to me.

THE PROTECTOR

There was no end to the mind games. Eric sometimes pitted me against his wife, Sharon. He was always taking me shopping to buy skimpy outfits to wear on our trips. This apparently made Sharon so jealous that, according to him, she and her friends were going to jump me one day.

He took me to the mall and sat me down at a table in the food court. This was supposedly the only place he could keep me safe. He left me there while he went to deal with Sharon, telling me not to move from that spot.

Eric came back a few hours later, saying he had calmed Sharon down. I was skeptical that the story was even real. He clearly just wanted to be seen as my protector. My tormentor, yes, but also my protector. I was supposed to believe that I needed him despite the constant torment.

This dynamic had some truth to it, though. This was never more evident than when we were on one of our trips. As scared as I was of Eric, I was far more scared of the men he left me with. You never knew how encounters with other men were going to go.

Eric took me to a dance club with him a few times. I had never been to one in my life since I liked alternative music growing up. I didn't know how to dance and had no interest in dancing with him. Thankfully, he just sat at the bar pounding beers and watching other people dance.

That wasn't too bad, so I didn't mind going back with him again. It certainly wasn't the scariest place he had taken me, not by a long shot! This time, though, things got weird. He took me into a private room in the back. He had me stand on the other side of the room while he chatted with men at the bar. He started sending them over to me, one by one. They weren't trying to dance. They just wanted to talk dirty, to flirt. But I was shy, and they were all drunk and gross. I didn't want to talk to them.

This upset Eric so much that he hurled a glass of beer at me. I dodged the glass, and it shattered against the wall behind me. The bartender started yelling at Eric, and we both were escorted out. We never went back, so I guess they banned him.

I never found out why he was sending those men over, but my hunch is that he was shopping me around to potential johns. Or maybe he just got a kick out of toying with me. Probably both. I never knew how it was going to go, whether he would leave me with these men. Whatever happened, I always feared the worst.

Eric was terrible, but he was a known entity. The men he left me with were not. Eric hadn't killed me, not yet. I didn't know what these strange men might do. He had told me about guys who would pay to kill women so they could have sex with the corpse. Again, this reminded me of the video and of the woman tied up in the warehouse.

These possibilities were so dark, so disturbing, that it was a relief when Eric came back after leaving me with other men. I had developed something like Stockholm syndrome. On the one hand, he had brought me to these horrible men, but who if not Eric would take me home? The very person who put me in danger was also my only ticket home, so I stuck close.

Eric emphasized his ability to "protect" me whenever he could. He treated me like his private property, which deserved a certain modicum of respect. For instance, he wouldn't let men "mark me up," which meant no cutting, no bruising. My white skin was insurance, he told me, as it made me a premium commodity for traffickers, and he wanted to keep it in pristine condition.

This sick combination of dependence on Eric and fear of him was why I sat so patiently on the stool in the rundown warehouse in Hailey, compliantly waiting for my trafficker to come back.

When he did, he was dragging a dolly behind him. He had me unload the cargo boxes, and then he loaded me back into the sleeper cab and went back into the office. I waited another hour for him to come back. The jingle of keys, the slam of the door, and the start of the engine. The truck lurched forward again. As usual, I was relieved not to be left behind. I had made it one more day, one more hour at the very least. I was that much closer to getting back home.

But it was only a short drive to our next stop, another seedy motel. I didn't ask why or what we were doing there; I already knew. I didn't run. I knew that Eric was right—I would never get away. I could see my whole future unfolding like this, forever. After four long months, it was hard to even imagine the life I had before this existence.

BREAKING AWAY

At the time, I had no way of knowing that this was my last trip with Eric. We returned home, and I went back to work at the bank on Monday. Life continued, and I had no reason to think things would ever change.

Unexpectedly, Eric showed up at my apartment one night demanding that I do him a favor. His boss at the trucking company had a truck that Eric wanted. He wanted me to negotiate the purchase because he wasn't confident he could close the deal on his own, on account of his poor English. He felt that a woman would get more favorable terms, as he assumed that everyone thought like him.

He had been teasing me with the idea for a while. He insinuated he would consider letting me go if I helped get him the truck. This was not a promise, not something he ever said outright, just something he hinted at. It was almost certainly another lie. I doubted that he had any intention of ever setting me free.

But I had to keep the faith. Desperate for a return to some kind of normal life, I was willing to try almost anything. I had already lost everything—my kids, my freedom, my safety, my autonomy. What else was there to lose?

There was a catch, though. I had to come up with $6,000 for a down payment on the truck. This was an impossible sum of money. In order to afford the child support I owed my ex-husband, Richard, I had started working at the bank, but I was only a few weeks into the job. I had nothing in savings. Some girls get paid by their traffickers. Not me. I never saw a dime of the money Eric made off me.

With no way to come up with that kind of money on my own, I had to turn to my parents for help. I called my father and explained the situation. This was difficult for me, considering our estrangement and his history of abusing me as a child. But my dad listened to my story, as much as I could bring myself to tell him given how ashamed I was. He agreed to wire me the money, no questions asked.

Now that I actually had the money, panic set in. Eric could not be trusted. He was a snake, an utter monster. He would simply take the money if he knew it was in my possession. I had to play my cards close to my chest. The money only gave me leverage as long as it was in my possession.

I told him I could *get* the money from my parents, not that I already *had* it. This was good enough for him. Eric gave me his boss's phone number and told me to set up the meeting.

A MAN YOU CAN TRUST?

The next day, I dialed the number.

"Is this Barry?" I asked meekly.

"Who's this?"

I introduced myself and asked to discuss a financial matter in person. Eric had told me Barry taught finance classes, so I said I had "a financial question." Barry was understandably hesitant and even suspicious. He wanted to know how I got his number. I explained I was "friends" with one of his employees.

"Well, you have a question," he said kindly. "Ask it."

This would not work. Eric had insisted that we meet face-to-face so I could work my womanly charms.

I emphasized how important it was to speak in person. Barry finally, hesitantly agreed. We made plans to meet at the local IHOP that Tuesday.

That night, I did research on the truck to determine its worth. I didn't know the first thing about big rigs or semi-trucks. I needed this deal to go through. Eric helped me rehearse my spiel.

The sun was still coming up when I arrived at the diner. My shift at the bank would start in a few hours. I was in my work clothes.

I pushed past the front door nervously. A well-dressed man was waiting at the hostess station. I was sure it was him. He stood out from all the other townies.

"Are you Barry?" I asked cautiously.

"Are you Julie?" he asked in reply.

We got a table and made chitchat. Our interactions were strained and formal.

Finally, Barry got down to business.

"So, what are we here to talk about today?"

This is when I finally broached the matter of the truck. Barry was confused about what role I was playing in this deal. I struggled to explain. I was saved when the waitress came to take our order.

My stomach was full of butterflies. I had no appetite—I hadn't had any appetite since the whole ordeal with Eric had begun. But Barry insisted we eat something. I ordered toast and nibbled at the corners over casual conversation.

Barry was nice. In fact, he was the first nice man I had spoken privately with in a long time. He actually seemed to take an interest in me, asking me questions. What did I do for work? For fun? I stammered something about liking mountains and the outdoors. It had been a long time since I had been around men with an interest in anything besides what they could do to my body.

Barry was trying to put me at ease. My hands were shaking. I was nearly incoherent.

Finally, we returned to the matter at hand. "So, you're here to talk about a truck?"

I started rattling off numbers, as I had rehearsed. I babbled something about the Kelley Blue Book value. I told him we had $6,000 to put down.

Barry listened patiently. When I was done, he spoke candidly. "Something seems wrong here. What's really going on?"

My jaw dropped. My whole body froze. This wasn't what I had rehearsed with Eric. We were off script.

"I'm sorry," he said earnestly. "Something just doesn't seem right."

He was so sincere and kind. His eyes bore right into me. I started to cry. He reached over and patted my arm gently.

Something inside of me broke. I had grown distrustful of all men, but something told me that I could trust this man. That I *should*.

So I opened up to him. I told him that I was actually in "a dangerous relationship" with his employee.

"Do you need help?"

I hesitated before nodding.

Barry said he couldn't help me unless I explained what was really going on.

This I couldn't quite do, not fully, not yet. I misrepresented the nature of the "relationship." Eric and I were not in a relationship and never had been, but I wasn't capable of conveying that I had been trafficked. I barely even had the words for what was happening to me. I didn't know what trafficking was. I felt immense shame over being a "sex worker," even if it was against my will.

When it was time for me to head back to work, I didn't want to go. I didn't want Barry to leave. He promised we would stay in contact.

"We'll get you to a safe place," he said. "We'll figure all this out."

We parted on those terms.

No sooner had I left the restaurant than I started freaking out again. What if Eric found out? There would be hell to pay. Eric often followed me around and spied on me. He could have been following me right then. I kept glancing over my shoulder and up and down the street on my way to work.

I also had reservations about trusting Barry. This situation was not so different from how Eric had entered my life. I had trusted him too. I no longer trusted my own judgment, not of men.

But I did have a good feeling about Barry—and I was desperate. I texted him an hour into my shift and asked if he texted.

He responded, "I do now."

We made plans to meet in the park for lunch.

I was looking over my shoulder the whole way to the park. It was a relief to see Barry waiting for me. As we began to stroll, I opened up a little bit more and hinted at how bad things really were, but I couldn't yet make myself tell him the whole truth. Still, I needed him to appreciate the true gravity of the situation.

Barry got the message. He insisted that we get me out of the apartment.

"It's not safe," he said. "Can you go to your parents' house?"

I wasn't sure. My parents had helped with the money, but we had no real relationship. Fleeing my current abuser to live with my past abuser wasn't exactly ideal. I didn't want to tell Barry any of this, so I promised to think about it.

We discussed how to handle Eric in the meantime. He would want to know how our conversation had gone. We devised a plan: Barry would make up an excuse for not wanting to sell the truck that wouldn't bring heat down on me.

"Call me if you need anything," he said before we parted. "I'm just a phone call away."

I walked back to work feeling better about having trusted Barry, but I was no less worried about Eric.

Barry didn't truly understand what Eric was capable of. I did.

I was afraid Eric would be waiting for me. Thankfully, I went home to an empty apartment. I had stolen Eric's key to my apartment days earlier when he wasn't looking. I had hidden the key under my mattress so he couldn't just waltz in like normal. But he could always kick down the door. I would have to just let him in.

It was only a matter of time before he showed up. I paced nervously in anticipation. I was worried he already knew what was happening from spying on me. What if he had seen me crying at the IHOP and the way Barry touched my arm? What if he had trailed us to the park? I was starting to think I had made a big mistake after all.

Eventually, the knock came. I got the door, and Eric didn't mention having to be let in. He was too focused on how the meeting had gone. I told him it was a no-go situation. In my nervousness, I let slip that Barry wouldn't take money coming from me—this was not part of the plan—but Eric didn't seem to notice this either. He seemed to have expected Barry to say no. It felt as though I had dodged a bullet.

Eric went to the bathroom in the master bedroom. The toilet flushed. When he came back, he told me to sit tight until he talked to Barry. He would let me know what our next move was.

After he left, I looked under the mattress for the key. It was gone.

CROSSING THE LINE

The next day, Eric dropped in on Barry at his office to talk about the truck. Barry said he wouldn't take the money and that the truck wasn't for sale. Eric must have not bought whatever reasons Barry offered and gotten suspicious. Barry and I had plans to meet for lunch at a place across the street from the bank. Eric must have found out because he called me later accusing me of sabotaging the deal. He said he knew all about Barry and me.

I denied everything. "We're just friends. He's nice to me."

"You're going to pay for this."

The phone went dead.

There would be no smoothing things over; I had crossed a line. I wasn't allowed to have friends. I wasn't even allowed to speak to other people. Seeing Barry, in secret, was unforgivable.

My only hope was that given Barry was Eric's boss, there would be enough leverage to get him off my back. Maybe he would just walk away from the situation to avoid getting fired or blacklisted. He had no way of knowing everything I had shared with Barry. Except Eric *did* know how afraid of him I was.

I called Barry and told him what happened. He said that we had to get me out of the apartment sooner, not later. It was too dangerous to stay by myself any longer. He was right, but I needed a few days to make arrangements with my parents. I had to pack my things. I had to get all my ducks in a row. If Eric figured out I was planning to leave immediately, he might do something to stop me. I needed to prepare and slip away quickly when it was time to go.

That evening at the apartment was nerve-wracking. I was terrified Eric would throw caution to the wind and come after me. I stayed up half the night worrying, but I eventually fell asleep.

I woke to the sound of the front door opening. It was still dark outside. I crept out of bed and tiptoed across the room. I took a deep breath and peeked out.

There was Eric, standing in the kitchen. Our eyes met and the world went gray. Time shifted into slow motion. Paralyzed with fear, I watched frame by frame as he came toward me. He struck me hard, with his fist maybe, or perhaps his whole body. I went flying backward and tumbled to the floor.

He had a knife in one hand. He was waving it around frantically and calling me names. *Whore. Bitch. Slut. Traitor. Traitor* was probably the worst in his mind. I had betrayed him.

He wanted to know exactly what I had told Barry. He was screaming. Terrified, I didn't know what to say.

"Nothing," I said. "Nothing!"

"Liar!"

He flung me onto the bed and started ripping my clothes off, literally ripping them to pieces. And he sodomized me. Brutally, horrifically, in a way I had never experienced. He had raped me so many times before, but never like this. He was absolutely brutal. He was trying to hurt me. Any concern about "marking me up" had gone out the window.

I pleaded with him to stop.

He held the knife against my neck and ran the blade across my face. "If you don't shut up it'll be worse."

This was the worst "punishment" I had ever received. He tortured me into the early hours of the morning. Literal torture. He went to the kitchen and came back with a jar of homemade hot peppers he kept at my place. He said they were straight from Mexico, habaneros or ghost peppers maybe, absolute fire. Eric bit into the peppers, releasing their juices before inserting them into me—it was painful enough that I wanted to die, but not painful enough that I blacked out. He wanted me to feel every visceral moment of torture. He had done this before. This time he wouldn't stop, wouldn't let me remove them. I was on fire from the pain. I felt like I was going to die.

When he was finally done with me, he walked away and left me sobbing on the bedroom floor. I listened for the back door to open and close before getting up.

I scrambled to find my phone and called Barry. I told him something terrible had happened. I could barely get it out through the tears.

"You move *today*," he said.

I called my parents and asked if I could come that day. They agreed to take me in. Barry stood guard while I packed and then drove me to their house.

I worried about putting my parents in danger. Eric had threatened to hurt them before, just as he had threatened my kids. They couldn't protect me from him—not really—and I couldn't protect them from him. But I had to get out of that apartment. I was out of time and out of options.

BREAKING AWAY

The next few weeks were surreal. I had actually made my escape. It took time for this new reality to sink in. It was hard to believe. In fact, I literally couldn't believe it. It felt as if things would fall apart at any moment. I was just waiting for the other shoe to fall.

Sleeping was hard. I was having recurrent nightmares about Eric coming to the house. The handle on the front door would start to turn and the door would creak open, just as it had on that fateful night at my apartment. I would jolt awake in a fright, gasping for air until I remembered where I was. *He doesn't have a key to my parents' house*, I reminded myself. *He can't get to me here.*

But it didn't feel that way, not at first.

Eric would not stop calling. He was calling Barry too. Barry had fired him. Eric blamed me, of course. He kept telling Barry that I had "tricked" him. Barry stopped answering. He told me to do the same, but my parents became irritated by the ringing. I finally picked up to try to get him to stop but could hardly get a word in edgewise. Familiar insults and threats bubbled up out of the receiver. He threatened to tell my ex-husband, Richard, that I was a whore and send him pictures of me with the men Eric had sold me to. Richard would be able to use these against me in our custody battle.

"You'll never get your kids back," he threatened. "You'll never get away from me."

Except I *had* gotten away. I was no longer in that apartment. For all his threats, Eric hadn't shown up at my parents' house.

Barry wanted to involve the police to make sure that he never did. My parents did not. They had their own secrets to keep and just wanted the problem to go away on its own.

I didn't want to involve the police either. Eric had convinced me that the police would arrest me for sex work if I ever went to them. He also had a friend on the local police force. He used to make me wait in the parking lot at the police station while they talked in the lobby. I watched while they shook hands and joked around. Eric wanted me to believe that the police were in his pocket.

Besides, the police had not been helpful in the past. When Richard raped me while we were still married, the police had said that filing charges would just get me branded a "man hater" and that no one would believe me anyway. They hadn't been helpful then. There was no reason to think they would be now.

Eric never did show up at the house. But the story didn't end there. He continued stalking me off and on for years—it was a constant worry. When I finally did go to law enforcement, the FBI warned that most "revenge scenarios" happen within the first two years. I was not out of the woods yet.

We stayed vigilant. We installed a state-of-the-art security system. I was careful about going out alone. I avoided places Eric might be. It would be several years before I was able to get a criminal injunction against him for stalking me. Another three years would pass before I testified against him. I didn't feel completely safe until he was deported.

Even today, I get the occasional niggling thought. What if he sneaks back across the border? What if he hires men to come after me? His friend and fellow trafficker Dog Man was still out there, as was Eric's rapist cousin, along with his sister, who would sometimes drive me to houses and warehouses to be trafficked. They were all still out there. So were all the other men who had raped and abused me. I had nightmares about all these people.

Yet slowly, slowly, the nightmares grew less frequent. Things got better. They weren't perfect, certainly not right away. My life was in shambles. My mental health was severely compromised. My problems were many. I still had to get my life back on track. I was locked in a nasty custody battle with Richard; I still had to work to get my kids back from him. I needed to figure out my career and how to trust and love again. This would all take time.

In those early weeks after breaking free, I did finally have a glimmer of hope about the future. My parents' house was not ideal, but it offered a level of safety. My job was going okay.

Barry was a positive presence in my life. I was working through my trauma. Things were looking up. I may have been looking up from the bottom, but I was looking up, nonetheless.

What had seemed impossible a few weeks earlier was now a reality. I had actually broken away!

THREE

HOUSE OF SECRETS

t's ironic that I escaped Eric by going back to my parents' house. My dad had given me the down payment on the truck so I could buy my freedom from Eric. When that hadn't panned out, he opened up his home to give me shelter. I had never been so thankful for anything in my life. But my childhood home was a house of secrets, and arguably where all my troubles began.

My parents were born in Idaho Falls. They could trace the family tree back through several generations in the area. It was the second biggest city in Idaho, which wasn't saying much. The city had the feel of a small town. People knew each other, especially within the Mormon community, which my family was part of.

The community could be described as insular, and my parents specifically tended to keep to themselves more than most. People thought we were weird. My parents rarely attended social gatherings outside of The Church of Jesus Christ of Latter-day Saints (LDS), and even the church they attended only sporadically. They floated in and out of the church, being hyper-observant at times only to start bad-mouthing the church a few months later. This cycle continued throughout my childhood, rinse and repeat.

They met in high school. My dad was dating my mom's cousin. My mom showed up at her house while he was over. My dad took a shine to her immediately and dumped the cousin. They started dating and got married right out of high school. This wasn't at all unusual for people in the Mormon community. We tended to marry young.

My parents were some of the first in their families to leave Idaho. My dad joined the military and became a military police officer in Washington, DC, so he and my mom moved to the East Coast.

This was hard on my mom. She was not well suited to city life. Her whole life was in Idaho. She missed the rolling mountains and quiet lakeside towns. The city intimidated her. It was loud. She didn't know how to get around. The traffic was abysmal in comparison to the wide-open roads of Idaho. Worst of all, she was thousands of miles from anyone she knew. Her whole family was on the other side of the country, and it took her some time to make friends at work.

By comparison, my dad acclimated well. City life suited him, as did the power of being a police officer. He quickly built camaraderie with the other MPs on his detail and often stayed out late drinking with them.

This, too, displeased my mom. He was coming home drunk all the time. She suspected him of flirting with other women at the bar. She knew how flirty he got while drinking. It tried her patience constantly, but she was nothing if not a patient woman.

Eventually, she had had enough. When my brother was born in 1974, she put her foot down and gave him an ultimatum. She was moving back to Idaho, with or without him. He could stay and be an officer or he could go to Idaho with his family. The choice was his, his family or the military, but he couldn't have both.

Surprisingly, he chose his family. He quit the military and returned to Idaho with her.

He would resent my mom for this for the rest of his life. My dad had loved his MP job, from which he had derived a sense of purpose, pride, and power.

His own father was a patriotic WWII veteran and former prisoner of war. He lost respect for my dad when he quit the military, for a *woman* of all things. He made no secret of this fact and shamed my dad regularly. He was always making comments and really rubbing it in.

My dad bristled at this criticism. He had always claimed his father to be abusive. My dad yearned for his respect but felt that getting it was a lost cause. My grandfather was short-tempered and unkind to my father, probably traumatized by war. My father didn't feel that understanding and generosity were in his father's wheelhouse.

You could say the same thing about my father—he tended to take his anger out on my mother. He blamed her for "making" him quit the military. He was always going on about how he had been close to making captain when she pulled the rug out from beneath him. This became part of our family lore, how my mother had ruined his life, repeated endlessly over meals and during fights.

My dad hated his civilian life. He moved the family to Utah to join his dad and brothers in the family business. The business had become successful when they moved it to the Salt Lake City area, where there was actually a potential customer base, but my dad hated working there. They installed central vacuum systems in homes and businesses.

"I'm a damn vacuum salesman," he was always saying, a reminder that my mother had made him give up a good military job to work in sales.

He was still holding that grudge when I came along in 1977.

THE BASEMENT

My childhood was a confusing one.

My family hopped between various Salt Lake City suburbs before eventually settling into the house I would grow up in, that house of secrets.

One of my first memories of early childhood is waking to my dad coming into my bedroom one night. I couldn't have been more than about three years old. I was in bed, wearing a little silk nightgown my grandmother had gifted me. My dad's mother appreciated the finer things in life, especially nice clothes. She got me embroidered silk pajamas every Christmas, which my dad made me wear.

My dad sat down close on the bed. He smelled funny in a way I couldn't pinpoint. I was too young to recognize the stale scent of cigarettes and too much alcohol. He pulled the blanket up over my head and off my lower half. Then he lifted up my nightgown and started touching me down below.

I was too young to understand this as well. Something about it felt wrong and naughty, but I couldn't have said why. This was my dad, after all. I wasn't supposed to question him. It hurt a little, but I didn't want to say so.

Unsure how to react, I laid completely still without making a peep, just waiting for it to end. He eventually stopped, pulled the blanket back down, and tucked me back in. He kissed me goodnight before leaving the room.

I didn't know what to think about what had happened. But I implicitly understood that this was something not to be talked about with anyone.

Nothing like this happened again for several years; or, if it did, I have repressed the memory. But when I was around age seven, my dad started taking me down into the basement.

This appeared innocent enough at first. My dad wanted to show me the money he was hiding from my mother down there. He kept cash rolled up inside a tube of PVC pipe with the ends capped. He used fishing line to lower the tube down into the basement walls through a hole in the ceiling. The basement was unfinished, which helped camouflage the crack in the ceiling and the little hook that kept the tube suspended behind the drywall.

You would never notice this setup unless you knew what to look for. I only knew about it because he regularly showed me the money. I watched as he fished the tube out of the wall. He took out the cash and splayed the bills in front of me. He let me feel them with my own hands.

The money was not a secret, only its location. He loved teasing my mom about the money. He made me swear not to tell her where it was hidden. It was our little secret.

This became a point of contention between my mom and me. My dad showed a favoritism toward me that made her jealous. The hidden money irritated her, but what really upset her was knowing that I had access to something she didn't. However badly she wanted the money, she resented that I had access to it even more. There was no reason for my dad to have even told her about the money except to hold it over her head.

My dad was always showing me the money in secret, so it was no surprise when he woke me one night to go down into the basement. We crept quietly down the stairs so as not to wake my mom. I leaned against the deep freezer, rubbing my eyes, waiting on him to fish the tube out of the wall. Except he didn't go for the money. He just looked at me funny and told me how pretty I was becoming.

"You're such a pretty little shit," he said. He was always calling me that. His *pretty little shit*.

My dad walked over and undressed me from the waist down. He started touching me between my legs.

This wasn't entirely shocking, as he had done it before. But I was older now, old enough for standing half-naked in front of my own dad to be embarrassing. My cheeks went red and steaming hot.

He kept talking the whole time he was touching me. "You're just so pretty now," he kept saying. "I just can't resist you."

I stood there frozen, pressing back hard into the deep freezer. Eventually, he stopped. "You're okay, right?"

I told him everything was fine. Of course, it wasn't. This was embarrassing. And I was getting sore down there. Also, it all felt wrong. I was supposed to trust my father, but this just didn't seem right.

Nothing about me must have looked fine, so we went back upstairs. He tucked me back in bed and that was that.

Only it didn't end there. His coming into my room at night and taking me down into the basement became a regular thing. We always crept quietly to avoid waking my mom. I learned which steps were creaky and to be avoided and which were safe. She never woke up anyway. She couldn't sleep without pills that knocked her out. A marching band couldn't have woken her up, never mind the delicate step of my tiny feet. I was only eight years old at the time and as light as a feather.

As the years passed, my dad took more and more liberties with my body. What started slowly kept escalating as he got braver and more comfortable with me.

He came home early from work one day while I was home alone. My brother and I were latchkey kids who walked home from school together. He would look after me until our parents got home in the evening, but he was off somewhere that day. My mom wouldn't be home for hours, as she never got off early from her job as a paralegal. My dad, however, set his own hours at the family business and could come and go as he pleased when it wasn't busy. Since we had the house to ourselves for a few hours, he took me down into the basement during the day.

This was the first time he leaned me over the deep freezer with my back to him. I didn't understand what was happening at first. All I knew is that it hurt much worse than usual. My body felt crushed under his. I remember my head banging against the freezer. I didn't understand that he was raping me from behind. It felt like he was going to kill me.

I wanted so badly to warn him. *He is going to kill me without even realizing it*, I thought. In my mind, there was no way he knew how badly this hurt. He was going to feel terrible when he saw what he had done. He would be so sad to find me dead. I wanted to warn him, but I was also afraid to upset him by saying how much it hurt.

He is going to kill me, and it is going to be all my fault. This made me feel terrible.

Afterward, my dad retrieved the tube of money from the wall. He let me keep several of the bills. I was a big girl now, old enough to have money of my own.

It would be years before I recognized the money for what it was—my compensation, my payment, my reward for my silence. He was buying me off.

DADDY'S LITTLE SHIT

This kind of thing went on for years. The sexual abuse started so early that it became normal for me. Other things my dad did were more upsetting, such as movie nights.

My dad started having me watch horror movies with him down in the basement at night. *Alien. The Shining. Predator.* My mom thought me far too young for these movies, but she didn't want to start a fight. She was always trying to avoid conflict. She might nag him that I was too young for R-rated movies, but she wasn't about to go to bat for me about anything.

Movie nights ran well past midnight, even on weeknights. They left me so tired the next day that I would fall asleep at school. The movies were frightening. I would cuddle up close and bury my face in my dad during the scary parts, which was maybe the point. It would explain why we only watched horror movies.

These weren't innocent daddy-daughter nights, of course. My brother and mom weren't invited, only me. He would touch and feel me during the movies, and afterward he would rape me. There wasn't a lock on the door, but no one came down to interrupt, as if they knew not to do so.

At the time, the movies were actually more upsetting than the abuse. They gave me nightmares. *The Shining* was the worst. I hated that Jack Nicholson's character goes mad and tries to murder his own family. This planted a fear in my head that my dad could do the same. He certainly had a big secret that he could bury with us.

I wouldn't be able to sleep after these movies. Sometimes, I crept into my parents' bedroom and tried to wake my mom, but she was always conked out on her sleeping pills. My dad would usually wake up first and kick me out of the room. Even if I was able to wake my mom, she would just mumble for me to go back to bed. She was too zonked out to offer any comfort.

So I would have to make the trek back to my room alone, looking over my shoulder and around corners for monsters hiding in the dark. I pulled the covers over my head to hide and was often still up when sunlight started coming through the window blinds. I used to scratch my nails on the shared wall separating my bedroom from my parents' room, hoping my mom would hear me and come save me.

To this day, I still have trouble sleeping, though it has more to do with the monsters that were out in plain sight.

At the time, I didn't think of my dad as a monster. I was less scared of him hurting me than I was of him hurting himself.

He sometimes brought a gun down with him into the basement. This was less scary than disturbing. I was terrified of him turning the gun on himself.

After molesting me or raping me, he would get emotional and start crying. He would pace around, talking to himself. Sometimes me, but mostly himself.

"I feel so bad."

"We shouldn't be doing this. I *know* that."

"I just can't help myself."

"I'm so attracted to you, and we just have this thing, you

and me. It's our thing, and nobody knows about it. This is just between us."

"It's not supposed to be there, but it is, and I can't help it."

He could go on like this for hours. It was hard to tell whether he was trying to justify his actions to himself or rationalize them to me. It was probably both. He did seem truly upset, but it's also clear he was manipulating my emotions.

He was always threatening to kill himself. One time, he put the gun in his mouth and threatened to pull the trigger.

"Daddy, no!" I cried. "Please, don't do this."

He took the barrel out of his mouth to speak. He said that it would be quick to shoot himself in the head. There was no other way, he had decided. He described what his brains would look like dripping down the wall, the back of his head blown open and his body slumped over.

We were both crying now. I pleaded with him not to do it. I told him what we were doing was fine. In fact, I even lied about *liking* it. It was "our thing," I said, parroting his words back to him.

None of this was true, especially not the part about liking it, but I was a kid who didn't want to watch her dad kill himself.

Still, saying the words made me feel even more responsible for what was happening to me. I had told him that I really liked what he was doing to me—who could blame him now?

I certainly didn't like what he was doing, but it was normal for me at this point. It's hard to convey how this kind of sustained abuse at a young age distorts your sense of reality. This was how I had grown up. You could argue that it was "our thing" in the same way that other kids' "things" might have been basketball or Girl Scouts. None of it was objectively normal, but it was *my* normal. It was all I had ever known.

MY BEST FRIEND

What did my mother think about all this?

You'd have to ask her. I never did.

She never came down into the basement to catch my dad with me, never interrupted daddy-daughter movie nights. This was surely by design, an intentional decision to be in the dark, so it's hard to know exactly what she knew. But I have no doubt that she knew something very wrong was happening.

My dad gave her plenty of reason to be suspicious. He was fairly open with how he treated me. We didn't talk about the worst of the sexual abuse, but he would act inappropriately out in the open. He used to have me take my shirt off in the house so he could run his hand up and down my back and tickle my chest.

"One day you're going to be too old for this," he would lament, "so we have to get it in now while we can."

He was always talking about how young and underdeveloped my body was, especially compared to my mother's. By his logic, this made what he was doing okay because I wasn't a *woman* yet.

"I'll never be too old for this," I would say, and I actually meant it.

Compared to our basement forays, this was actually one of the least weird ways my dad showed his "affection." It didn't seem so bad. I knew it was unusual, and not to be discussed out of the house, but it seemed like a normal sign of affection. My dad tickled me and rubbed my back. Of course, I would never be too old for that—it would have been like him saying I would someday be too old for a hug or a kiss goodnight. In my world, it was normal.

My mother did not agree.

"She's getting too old. She can't just be taking her shirt off."

"She has a brother in the house, you know."

"Brian, she is your *daughter.*"

Nagging him to stop just egged him on more. My dad got off on showing her that he could do whatever he wanted with me. Flaunting it was clearly part of the fun. He teased her with my body just as he teased her with the hidden money.

My dad played us off each other. He would bring home lingerie for her and hold it in front of my body. Sometimes he even took me with him to the lingerie store.

"This would look better on your mother," he would say, cupping his hands under his own chest to insinuate cleavage. "She'll fill it out better."

I was only twelve at the time, a late bloomer who wouldn't hit puberty for another three or four years.

This made my mom upset and even jealous. I doubt that she ever wore this lingerie. She hated knowing that I had helped pick it out. It disgusted her.

Still, she often took out her anger on me instead of him. Our relationship became ever more competitive and even combative. When she took me shopping, as she often did, she would make petty comments about the clothes I selected.

"Excuse me, you want to wear *that*?"

"You only want that to show off your figure."

"Look how sheer that is. You *want* men to see straight through it."

It was clear that *men* meant my dad. It wasn't as if I was dating boys from school, not yet. The church strongly encouraged no dating until you were sixteen.

There wasn't even anything particularly scandalous about the clothes I picked out. They weren't skimpy or provocative. They were just normal clothes from the department store. I was becoming more interested in fashion as I got older, but she seemed to think the outfits were supposed to attract my dad.

What she thought didn't matter, though, because I had my own money from the basement to purchase what I wanted to wear. I had been squirreling it away for years. I didn't know the value of it when I was younger and just hid it in my room. As I got older, the money all went toward clothes. I took it from my dad and spent it with my mom.

My mom didn't have to permit this—she didn't have to take me shopping or let the cashiers ring me up. She could have taken the money away. She didn't want to rock the boat, so she just stewed silently in anger and jealousy.

This jealousy betrayed her knowledge of our "secret." She knew where the money was coming from. She knew exactly what was going on—if not the sordid details, at least the general shape and outline. But it was preferable to pretend that she didn't.

I know that none of this was easy on my mother. I won't excuse her complicity, but she clearly struggled with what was happening. Like my father, she often talked about killing herself.

When she drove me to school in the mornings, she would sometimes say that she might not be able to pick me up later.

"You'll have to find another way home. I might go drive off a cliff."

"Mom. You can't do that."

"I just can't live like this anymore," she would say, her voice breaking. "This isn't how I want to live."

I would spend the whole school day worrying that I would never see her again.

Sometimes, she talked about running away. She wanted to leave and never come back. It was a sentiment I could under-stand, but I didn't want her to abandon the family. My brother and I were cloistered in the house, isolated and only allowed to have one friend each, and even those friends were not really wel-come at the house. I needed my mom.

According to her, she was my best friend. "Mothers are always best friends with their daughters."

I had no reason to believe this wasn't true, no way to really even verify the statement. I was so sheltered and impression-able that I immediately believed her. I had no way of knowing what a best friend looked like. She said we were best friends, so it must be true.

AGING OUT

By fifteen, I was on the cusp of puberty. At long last, this gave my dad pause.

He took off my shirt one day and started tickling me. But something seemed different about him when he flipped me over. He hesitated.

"You know what, you *are* too old for this," he said. He told me to put my shirt back on.

This came as a shock. I pulled my shirt back over my head and curled into a ball. I didn't understand what I had done to upset or offend him.

Not long afterward, he sat me down and said that I was too old for what we were doing down in the basement.

And just like that, the sexual abuse stopped. My dad was still emotionally abusive. He wasn't always appropriate around me and made comments he shouldn't have, but the touching and the feeling stopped. There were no more movie nights, no more sneaking off to the basement—all of it stopped, cold turkey, as if a switch had been flipped.

This was a confusing shift for me to absorb. You would think a celebration was in order, as I had never liked what my father was doing to me, no matter what I had once said. Instead, I felt rejected and cast aside. As grotesque as it was, the abuse had been the basis of our whole relationship. When it came to an abrupt stop, I blamed myself. I didn't understand what I had done wrong.

It was only after I had some distance from it, months later, that my father's abuse began to upset me. I was suddenly infuriated all the time. My brother and I had always been good kids. We behaved ourselves; my dad made sure of that. Growing up, we were punished harshly for stepping out of line, so we didn't. But then I felt rebellious. I was nearly bursting with pent-up rage.

The only outlet I had was music. It was the nineties and I had discovered grunge. The angst and detached anger of the genre spoke to me. I would blare Pearl Jam songs on the big speaker system in my room at full blast until my dad told me to knock it off. I would nudge the volume down a notch, only to turn it back up a few minutes later. This was my one little act of rebellion and defiance. It was my way of screaming at my father for what he had done to me, at my mother for what she had let him do. I didn't have the nerve to confront them directly.

Unsurprisingly, this outlet was an insufficient release valve for my anger. As I grew angrier about what he had done to me and what she had allowed to happen, I began to despise myself for letting them do it. I thought about all the times I had told my dad it was okay, even said that I *liked* it. It was sickening. It was pathetic.

A couple of years before, my brother's best friend, Nick, died by suicide after a girl dumped him. He called her up and shot himself in the head with his father's gun while she was still on the line. He was a cute boy I had crushed on, so his death came as a big shock. I didn't dwell on it at the time. It was only later that I realized I could do the same.

This was a major revelation. There was *always* a way out. Nick had tasted life and said, "Nope, not for me," and checked himself out. Who would have thought it possible? You could just opt out! No one could make you stay and live your own life. You could end it at any time. What a relief!

Thoughts of suicide were a huge comfort. You could stick a gun in your mouth and blow your head off whenever you wanted. Who would care? Not me. My brains would be running down the back of the wall, as my dad had so colorfully explained. I wouldn't have a care in the world like that. This must have been why my mom and dad were always threatening suicide.

At the age of sixteen, I devised a plan to kill myself. When the time was right, I would shoot myself with my dad's gun, just like Nick. I wrote a "goodbye, cruel world" note and everything. It didn't mention the sexual abuse—even in death I couldn't face up to that, couldn't out my dad. The note hardly even mentioned him. It talked about *me*. I wrote about how I couldn't handle things, that everything was so messed up and too much to bear. It not only let my parents off the hook completely, but it let me off the hook too. I didn't have to verbalize what had happened, that the abuse and all the secrecy and distortions and enabling around it were what actually felt like *too much*.

I filed the note away in a folder and hid it in my room. There was comfort in just having it on hand. I had crossed my t's and dotted my i's and would be ready to go when the time came. I could check out at any time.

For the first time in my life, I had the power to make a decision that was entirely up to me, even if it meant taking my own life.

FOUR

BOYS

My dad had his reasons for putting an end to sexually abusing me when he did. Age really did have something to do with it. Since I had turned fifteen, I would soon be old enough to start dating in the Mormon community. Boys would have an actual reason to take interest in me.

This couldn't just be ignored. Dating was serious business in our circles. It wasn't unusual for high school sweethearts to tie the knot after graduation. My dad's "thing" with me would soon run up against my need to start thinking about marriage and my future. So of course he had to cut it off. Otherwise, the disruption it would likely have caused might have brought down unwanted attention on us.

I went on my first date within days of turning sixteen. The date wasn't my idea or my doing. Dating held little interest for me. I just wanted actual friends. My only real friend, Sara, had been asked out on a date by a boy she wasn't particularly into, and she didn't want to go out with him alone. So she decided to make it a double date by setting me up with his friend, a boy named Sean. In any event, group dates were more acceptable for people our age.

I only went on the date to make Sara happy, as part of my pattern of always putting other people's wants before my own. This was especially true of my relationship with men, which is why I started dating Sean despite actively disliking him.

My affinity for him, or lack thereof, did not matter. I had no sense of agency or self-interest. I just wanted to make sure other people got what they wanted. My self-esteem was entirely reliant on meeting other people's needs and suppressing any of my own desires. My dad's abuse had conditioned me to give men— or now, boys—what they wanted. Sean wanted me, and so of course he could have me—whether or not I liked him. *Any* boy, or man for that matter, could have made me his by merely asking. They didn't even have to ask. It could just be assumed.

FIRST DATE

Although I was now old enough to date, sexual activity was still strictly forbidden. The LDS church drilled this into our heads. No sexual contact of any kind until marriage. No sex, no petting, no touching, no heavy kissing. Physical contact beyond a hug goodnight or a peck on the lips was not allowed.

As I understood it, there was no greater sin than premarital sex. We were lectured extensively on the matter in Sunday school. My teacher would try to scare us by telling us that premarital sex was worse than murder. We had more to fear than just pregnancy or sexually transmitted diseases. Our very souls were at stake. Having sex out of wedlock meant eternal damnation.

This quickly became a problem in my life. Sean moved fast. He tried to kiss me on the first night out, and of course I let him. He could have done more. He could have done anything. I had absolutely no sense of boundaries or bodily autonomy given how my father had treated me. I had already agreed to go on the date. In my mind, this was akin to handing over the keys to my body. I was his now. He was free to do as he wanted with me.

We never had "real" sex, no actual intercourse, but we did other things that made me worried about the state of my soul. Sean played fast and loose with the church rules, putting his hand up under my shirt or under the waistband of my underwear. With clothes still on, he would lie on top of me and grind against my body. Anything we could do with clothes on was fair game in his book. We weren't *really* having sex unless our clothes were off. I didn't know whether this was *technically* sex, but it was enough to make me feel guilty and worry about going to hell.

Sean's rationalization wasn't very convincing, but I wanted to believe. *Maybe it isn't really sex as long as we have our clothes on.* How was I to know what was and wasn't sex? I had no sexual experience outside of my father having abused me, but I didn't see that as sex at all. That was just my *dad's* "thing," not mine. The church warned against sex and *lust*. I certainly felt no lust for my father. Whatever he had done to me (which I was in denial about even having happened), it was certainly not sex. As strange as it might sound, I honestly thought of myself as a virgin. And if that wasn't sex, well, maybe this wasn't either.

This kind of denialism made me terribly naive about sex. The first time Sean orgasmed while grinding on me, I was surprised and horrified for him. *Oh, my god*, I thought, *he peed himself!* I pretended not to notice so he could save face. Despite everything my father had subjected me to, I didn't understand the physicality of sex. I had tuned all that out while it was happening and then tried to contort it into normalcy to deny it had ever taken place.

This kind of poor rationalization could only get me so far. Deep down inside, I knew what we were doing. I knew that, according to the church, it was wrong. I worried about being found out and ostracized. There was a girl in our school who had gotten pregnant, and her parents had moved her into the garage to sleep on a cot between the cars. I didn't want to become like her.

Most of all, I worried about going to hell. The guilt and fear eventually became too much to bear.

"I have to talk to the bishop about what we're doing," I told Sean one day.

He shrugged. "Go ahead. I'm not doing anything wrong, but if *you* need to talk to him, go ahead."

He wasn't as agreeable as this sounds. His tone was defiant. He was daring me to admit what we had done to the bishop. He knew that I wouldn't; I wasn't that brave. I had been conditioned into passively accepting abuse, and I was resigned to letting Sean have his way, my own soul be damned.

Did I fear the repercussions? The wrath of God? Very much. But I didn't feel any sense of autonomy. It wasn't in my hands.

Not everyone was so willing to break the rules. Some kids took church doctrine very seriously. Sara was among them. She was a "good girl." I envied her for this. I wanted to be like her, but it wasn't in my power to turn boys down. I didn't want to have sex. I didn't want to break the rules. I just couldn't assert myself and say no. I would sooner burn in hell forever than tell a man no—to go to hell for a boy like Sean, a boy I not only didn't like, but also actively *disliked*.

Sean was not a good person. He was selfish and quick to anger. He once hit Sara for "talking back." She was uncomfortable with us making out in the back seat of the car. She didn't want to be around people breaking the rules. Sean told her to stop nagging. When she kept saying we needed to get going, he reached into the front of the car and slapped her hard across the face.

Sara was speechless. So was I. Literally. I said nothing while he went back to making out with me.

Who was I to tell him no?

I let him do what he wanted to me while listening to Sara cry in the front seat.

MATCHMAKER

Things didn't last long with Sean.

Sara eventually broke up with her boyfriend and moved on to another boy named John. Sean was now superfluous and unnecessary. Sara certainly didn't want him around after he had clocked her in the face. Sara was the only reason we were even together. So when she stopped inviting him along to things, that was fine by me. It was just her and John and me now.

This presented its own problem, though. I was back to being the third wheel.

Sara made it her mission to remedy this situation as quickly as possible. John had a friend she wanted to set me up with, some guy named Richard. Though our age, Richard worked in the produce section at the grocery store.

"We should all hang together," Sara said. "Wouldn't that be so fun?"

She was clearly trying to set me up on a date, never mind that I was still technically seeing Sean. It didn't matter to her, though, so it didn't matter to me either. I had been seeing less and less of him anyway.

John drove Sara and me to meet Richard at the grocery store. We waited in the parking lot for him to go on break. The grocery doors eventually opened. Richard stepped outside and scanned the parking lot. John waved him over. He skulked across the parking lot and hopped into the back seat of the car with me.

Richard gave me a nod. I said hey. I sat quietly while they all talked. Sara had to keep steering the conversation back to me. She wanted Richard and me to engage more, but I had difficulty making small talk and was reserved.

Richard was not. He was loud and boisterous. Our personalities clashed. I found him completely off-putting right from the start. He seemed snotty, mean-spirited. He talked about people behind their backs. He uttered crude jokes that made me uncomfortable. Everything about him gave me a bad feeling in the pit of my stomach. To make matters worse, I was not attracted to him at all—his nose was too big and his laugh irritating.

None of that mattered. I knew we were still going to have to start dating. Sara was not going to let it go.

When Richard went back to finish his shift, Sara turned around to face me. "What do you think? He's cool, right?"

"Yeah, he seems cool," I lied.

"You like him, right?"

I shrugged and said he seemed fine.

This was good enough for Sara. She insisted that we come back and see him again.

As usual, what I wanted didn't matter. She needed someone to go on double dates with her, someone who wasn't Sean. Richard and I were the most convenient option.

I can't be too hard on Sara for this. We were only sixteen, just kids. She didn't know how awful Richard would turn out to be. I should have been able to just say no, I didn't want to date him. It wasn't her fault that I was constitutionally incapable of doing so.

They took me back to the grocery store to see Richard several more times. Sara kept inviting him along on group outings. I never took to Richard any better, which is to say not at all. Our conversations never got better or easier, but it was clear that we were *supposed* to be a thing now.

We weren't actually dating, though. If Sean was fast, Richard was decidedly not so. I couldn't even tell if he was interested in me. Sometimes it seemed like he was, but he could also be standoffish, even cold. He would be flirting one minute and giving me the cold shoulder the next. Sometimes, he would only talk to Sara and John, as if I weren't even there.

Without Sara's playing matchmaker, we might not have ever started dating. She kept forcing the issue.

"Has he asked you out yet?"

"Are you guys official?"

"Why doesn't he ask you out already? What's the problem?"

I would just shrug and say that I didn't know. She pushed me to be more proactive. She thought I should make it clear how much I *really liked him*. Of course, I didn't like him, but I didn't have the heart to tell her that.

Being proactive wasn't my style. I wanted to do it to make her happy, yet I literally couldn't do something so aggressive. If she needed me to ask him out, she would be waiting forever. I would have dated any boy in front of me, even Richard, but they were going to have to make the first move.

Given that I didn't want to date Richard, but also couldn't turn him down, I prayed that he never would. I hoped he would eventually lose interest, if he had any to begin with. I wished that Sara would drop the whole idea. I hoped she and John would just break up.

No such luck. After a month of Sara's playing matchmaker, Richard finally called the house to ask me on a date, just the two of us.

My heart sank. Hanging out with him around Sara and John was one thing. Hanging out alone was going to be horrible.

"Sure," I said. "Of course."

We met for dinner. That's all it took. We were official—a real couple, exclusive, as far as I knew, and there was nothing I could do about it.

NEW BOY, SAME STORY

Dating Richard meant cutting things off with Sean. But breaking up with someone was also not something I had it in me to do. I was afraid of hurting anyone's feelings, particularly those of any male who had shown any interest in me.

My solution was to stop taking or returning Sean's calls. The phone would ring and ring. If my parents answered, I told them to say I wasn't home.

Sean wouldn't take the hint. He started stalking me. He had caught word that Richard and I were a thing now and wanted to catch us together on a date. He would dress up from head to toe in hunting camo and hide in the bushes outside my house. We caught him doing this not once, but twice.

Richard was at the house the second time, along with Sara and John. Richard spotted Sean out in the bushes, peering in through the basement windows.

"What the hell?" Richard said, looking at me in disbelief.

John and Sara started laughing. Richard went outside to confront Sean. He told him to get lost and not come back unless he wanted a pummeling. Sean slunk off, tail between his legs.

The whole thing was absolutely ridiculous. Two boys were fighting over me, and I didn't want to be with either one of them.

Richard was no better than Sean. He was just as mean and even more controlling. He treated me like an inconvenience. It was as if going out with me were some kind of favor for which I should be thankful.

Richard continued to vacillate in the amount of interest he showed in me. Sometimes days or weeks would go by without his returning my phone calls. Then he would call again and act as if nothing had happened.

This behavior was baffling at the time. *Does he like me or not?*

It was only much later that I recognized this emotional manipulation for what it was. Richard was flexing his power over me. He wanted to make it clear that it was me who needed him, not the other way around. He could disappear at any time, so I'd better get it together and do what he wants.

That Richard was mean and controlling didn't strike me as particularly noteworthy. In my mind, this was just how men were. My dad was a short-tempered bully, as was Sean—of course Richard would be too. All men operated on a hair trigger, or so I thought. This was just how men treated their girlfriends, wives, sisters, all women. It was just the way things were. I didn't like it, but I wouldn't have questioned it any more than a dog chasing a cat. It was the natural order of things.

This was nonsense, of course. I should have known better. It's not like there weren't other boys I could have dated, nicer boys. My brother's best friend had a crush on me. He was only three years older. We could have dated. I knew this.

He even told me he wanted to marry me someday, but I was already spoken for by then.

My whole life might have been different if I had dumped Richard for him, but this didn't seem like a real option at the time. Richard had already chosen me. How I felt about him didn't factor into the equation. What I wanted was completely immaterial, as always.

Growing up, I had been allowed no choice about what happened to my body, not from my earliest memory of my dad coming into my room that night and pulling the blanket up over my head. I was conditioned as a child to give men what they wanted without resistance or ruckus. It wasn't that I struggled to weigh my desires against theirs. Mine simply did not matter. I had been taught that what I felt was irrelevant.

This conditioning kept me passive and compliant, under Richard's control right from the start. I didn't fear him, not yet. I just couldn't bear to step out of line and hurt his feelings. Richard repelled me but pleasing him mattered more than anything. Actually leaving him was so out of the question in my mind that I would do anything possible to stay on his good side.

Since I was stuck with Richard, I did my best to stay positive about the relationship. I looked for silver linings. It wasn't easy, as Richard had few redeeming qualities. He was ugly in every way imaginable, inside and out. But we were a couple. He could, very occasionally, be sweet or sentimental. We called each other "bubbo" for short and spoke in a kind of baby talk we termed "bubbonics." It was a shared language with secret words, a kind of inside joke. We liked the same music and the same nineties fashions. I respected him for being a hard worker who put in long hours at the grocery store. He would skip hanging out with us on his breaks if the store was busy.

None of this was enough. We were a couple, not bandmates or coworkers. Being a good employee didn't make him any less of a shitty boyfriend.

But what could I do? I was already trapped. There was nothing to do but put on a smile and try to make the best of a bad situation.

Would my life have turned out better if I could have mustered some self-respect, some sense of agency, and dumped him?

You might as well ask whether my life would have turned out better if my dad hadn't raped me. Of course it would have, but follow this line of reasoning back far enough and you're wondering, *would I be better off never having been born?*

Which, as it so happened, was often how I felt.

SOMETHING OLD, SAME THING NEW

Dating Richard gave me a short reprieve from worrying about eternal damnation. He moved much slower than Sean. We didn't have sex. We didn't even hold hands. He loathed physical displays of affection. Five months passed before he even tried to kiss me.

This came as a surprise. I expected him to be just like Sean, or my father for that matter. That he wasn't actually had the effect of making me feel inadequate. *What's wrong with him? Shouldn't he be all over me?*

It wasn't clear why Richard waited so long to make a move. He was clearly interested in things of a sexual nature. He was always commenting on my body in ways that made me feel uncomfortable. He would assess the size of my chest, the amount of fat on my arms and thighs, the contours of my face. He was always talking about sexual things. I even caught him looking at pornography on several occasions, which was upsetting. But for some reason, he didn't make sexual advances.

My theory now is that Richard was testing me. This was his way of making sure I wasn't the kind of girl who made moves. If I was the kind of girl who would sleep with him, then maybe I was the kind of girl who would sleep with someone else too. (I never told him about the things Sean did to me, despite his prying questions. I denied everything. It wasn't something I was capable of discussing.)

I wasn't complaining about the situation, though. I didn't even want to be physical with Richard. He was unattractive to me in every possible way. I would have been happy to stay platonic or celibate forever. It was a relief not to be violating church doctrine anymore.

Unfortunately, it didn't last.

Five months into dating, Richard made a big deal about our first kiss. We went out to a diner that served root beer floats and hung old-fashioned décor on the walls. He picked me up in his Corvair. The whole thing felt like an episode of *Happy Days*.

It was all a little cheesy, but also pleasantly sweet. Richard was rarely so sentimental. He didn't like to "act the part" of a boyfriend. He was a militant nonconformist and contrarian. He liked alternative music and fashion. Anything that was popular was lame, anything expected of him onerous, and he flouted those expectations whenever possible. Boyfriends are supposed to hold hands with their girlfriend? Well, then he was going to be the boyfriend who didn't hold hands.

In retrospect, the whole night was strange. Richard likely had ulterior motives that had little to do with being sweet.

His relationship with his family was very strained. His mom and stepdad had kicked him out of the house. They were barely on speaking terms at the time. He never shared anything with them about his life, so it was notable that he did tell them about his plan for our big date, that this would be our first kiss. This was his way of making us official. His parents were super excited for him, which was probably the point. I had a tiny part as the love interest in his redemption story.

It wasn't long after our first kiss that the question of sex came up. And I do mean literally: Richard came right out and asked me if I wanted to have sex.

I was caught off guard. "Is that what you want?"

"Yeah, I really do."

"Okay. Yeah, of course."

I didn't actually want to have sex with Richard, but it was nice to be *asked*. It was stunning, even. Sean had never asked. He simply did what he wanted with my body, as had my father. The fact that someone would ask for permission before touching me was new territory.

Regardless, I didn't actually feel capable of saying no, so it wasn't really a choice. Maybe Richard knew that at the time, maybe not.

Richard was staying with his grandparents since his mother had thrown him out of the house. His grandparents gave him a bedroom in the basement. He would sneak me in through the window so we could fool around without them knowing.

In my mind, this was technically my first time having "real" sex. What my father had done to me was nonconsensual, so I didn't (and still don't) think of it as sex. I thought of myself as a virgin.

That stuff with Sean: well, we had our clothes on, right?

That thing with my dad? He was my dad—you can't have sex with your dad.

I had convinced myself that sleeping with Richard was going to be my first time. When we actually started having sex, it was like, *Oh my god, it's just this?*

He likes to do this too.

I was heartbroken. It was a horrifying revelation. Sex was *this*.

My delusions about what my dad had done to me started to unravel. The walls came crumbling down.

His "thing." Our "thing." It was just this. *This.*

The truth was too much to bear. I could only respond with even more denialism. I told myself that all that business with my dad had never even happened. It must have been a misunderstanding. False memories. Anything but this.

And so, just like that, I rewrote the story of my childhood. My father and I had simply been close. It was a normal relationship. All that stuff I had imagined was just that, a figment of my imagination.

FIVE

MY LIVE-IN BOYFRIEND

ichard moved into our house when I was only seventeen. His mom had kicked him out not long before we met, after she came home one day and caught him with his hands up his female neighbor's shirt. Richard was only fifteen at the time, but this girl was practically a child.

That was the last straw. Not long before this incident, Richard had gotten into a terrible fight with his stepdad. Richard started throwing punches while his mom screamed in the background. His stepdad fended him off a bit before deciding enough was enough. He picked Richard up and tossed him to the ground.

This was not the first time Richard had been caught eyeing young girls. His mom had caught him spying on his half-sisters while they were getting dressed. There was also an incident with a younger cousin. I don't know what the allegation was; Richard wouldn't tell me. He claimed they were blowing things way out of proportion. He didn't want to talk about something that "didn't happen."

Whatever "didn't happen" with the cousin had taken her years of therapy to get over. Her parents, his aunt and uncle, wrote him off completely. They wouldn't come to family functions if he was going to attend.

Now his mom was writing him off too. She told him to pack his things and get out.

PEACEMAKER, CARETAKER

Richard went to stay with an aunt and uncle. They let him stay in their basement until his mom pressured them to kick him out. She wanted him to have to come groveling back to her. He was a minor and still her responsibility. The way Richard saw it, she had only thrown him out of the house to show him his place. Her house, her rules.

Eventually, the aunt and uncle buckled and told Richard he couldn't stay there forever; it was time for him to return home. Richard wouldn't go home. He went to his grandparents and begged them to let him stay there. They agreed to let him stay on a cot in the basement.

His grandmother kept pressuring him to make amends with his mom, but Richard wouldn't so much as talk to his mom or stepdad.

When Richard and I started dating, his family began using me as their go-between. I was both liaison and peacemaker. They were always asking me to relay information for them. They hoped I could get him to "see reason."

Richard didn't see reason. He blamed them for severing the relationship. I could see both sides, but I always took his. That was my nature—I wasn't going to challenge a man.

Richard did have a point. His mother was controlling and mean. She could be emotionally abusive, which definitely affected how he turned out. His mom never liked him. His father left shortly after he was born, and she seemed to blame Richard for her failed marriage. Richard felt that his mom had held a grudge against him from the time he was a little baby. He was a constant reminder of what had gone wrong in her life. It was clear to him that she favored the children she had with her second husband. I thought Richard was exaggerating all of this at first. He was not. I saw it with my own eyes. She was really nasty to him. He wasn't reasonable, but neither was she.

I still wanted to help them mend the relationship and bring the family back together. This was a role I was accustomed to. I had spent my whole childhood trying to keep my parents united. My dad was always yelling at my mother for something. I thought of myself as the glue that held them together. When they fought, it felt like my fault. If one of them had left the marriage or died by suicide, that would have been my fault too.

Keeping my parents together was an incredibly stressful responsibility that no teenager should have to bear. Now add to that burden the responsibility of managing Richard and his family—it was a lot of weight for a teenager to carry. But I didn't want Richard to become totally estranged from his family. I had to keep the peace. I had to be the glue.

I worked on Richard on the sly. He had forbidden me from speaking with his family. I took their calls when he was away at work. I suggested we visit them in ways that might be more amenable to him. I told him we should cut them some slack and be the "bigger person."

Richard wasn't having any of it. He didn't want to visit. He had no interest in mending the relationship. He was too stubborn to admit wrongdoing, and he had no material reasons to do so. As long as he had his job at the grocery store and a place to crash, he didn't have to submit to his mom's rules.

His mom understood this, which is why, when my diplomatic efforts weren't working, she convinced the family to cut him off. She pressured his grandparents and uncle to turn him away. She thought this would force him to come home and change his behavior.

No dice. Richard started sleeping in his car instead.

I was furious with his family because they had just given up on him entirely. I cut off contact with them too. They could kick rocks and find another middleman, as far as I was concerned.

At night, Richard started parking his car at the end of a dead-end street near my house. I sneaked out blankets from the linen closet and food and sodas from our fridge. We hung out under the blankets in the back seat of his car. It was so cold that our breath turned to frost on the windows. I felt so bad for him.

After a few days of this, the weather took a turn for the worse. I explained the situation to my parents and asked them if he could stay with us.

I wasn't expecting my dad to say yes—but he did.

Richard moved into our basement that same day.

This was the same basement where my father had abused me. They had finished half the basement since then, adding a computer room and guest room. Richard stayed in the guest room. When I went down there, I had to walk by the door to the deep freezer where that whole nightmare with my father had unfolded. When this inevitably triggered bad memories, I would push them out of my mind by whatever means possible, including self-harm, and keep on with life as usual. It was the only way I could function.

Inviting Richard into the house was a decision I quickly came to regret. I already felt trapped in the relationship. Richard monitored my movements and who I interacted with. Now that we were under the same roof, I had no escape, no reprieve. He could keep tabs on me 24/7. He knew my every movement. No one could call the house without his knowledge. I couldn't go out with friends without him finding out. I rarely even saw Sara anymore. It was just Richard and me all day long. The only time I was free from him was when he was at work. Even then, he would call the house while on break just to check up on me.

Looking back, Richard clearly manufactured the situation. He knew I would take him in and take care of him. There was a reason he had parked down the street from my house. There was a reason he invited me into the car. We could have just hung out at my house where it was warm. He wanted me to see how he was living. I had a mother's instincts; it was cold out, and there was no way I was going to let him live in a car. He knew this and exploited my caring nature. In so doing, he not only avoided submitting to his mother's power play but also managed to monitor me ever more closely, killing two birds with one stone. And I fell for it hook, line, and sinker.

KEEPING UP APPEARANCES

It was my dad who said that Richard could stay with us. My mom didn't want him in the house. She liked him but worried what the neighbors would think, since it might look improper for Richard and me to live under the same roof.

My mother always cared about keeping up appearances, first and foremost. When I was about nine or so, someone broke into the house while my brother and I were home alone. We heard the front door open and shut. Our parents weren't supposed to be home for several hours. We called out for them, but no one answered. Heavy footsteps echoed up the stairs. It didn't sound like either of our parents.

We hid in the basement and listened as the footsteps moved from room to room upstairs, followed by the sound of drawers opening and slamming shut. Then we heard the back door open. We took the opportunity to run up the stairs and out the front door. We went to the neighbors' house across the street and called 911.

The police came and cleared the house with guns drawn. They confirmed signs that someone had been in the house. Drawers were left open upstairs, but strangely nothing was missing. My mom showed up while they were still doing their report. She barely registered that there had been a break-in but was absolutely mortified to have police in the house.

After the cops left, she scolded us for calling the police with the house a mess. She was embarrassed to have "people" in the house with the beds unmade and stuff out on the floor. Oddly, she cared more about how things looked than making sure we were okay.

Having your teenage daughter's boyfriend move into the house was not a good look, not in our community. People from the church already thought our family was weird and having him there was just one more strike against us.

My brother didn't like the idea of Richard in the house either, but he had just returned from a two-year mission in Canada that had left him humbled and noncombative. He didn't challenge my parents about taking in Richard.

As a family, we handled the situation the same way we handled everything else—denialism. My parents treated Richard like just another kid, as if they had adopted him. They ignored the obvious reality that Richard and I were in a relationship. This kind of cognitive dissonance was normal in our house.

My mom wasn't going to challenge my dad on letting Richard live with us. Whatever my dad said was how things went, always. She remained worried, though, so she did her best to keep Richard out of sight. Out of sight, out of mind, or so she hoped.

My parents were in the market for a cabin at the time. They would leave us at home for extended weekends while they looked at properties. My mom told us to stay away from the windows and to keep the blinds drawn. She didn't want the neighbors seeing Richard and me alone in the house. She did everything she could to avoid drawing attention to us.

Unfortunately, Richard did not. He bullied the neighborhood kids all the time. He pushed a boy half his age off a bike because he thought the kid had a crush on me. Controlling and neurotic, Richard always thought everyone had a thing for me.

The neighbors started complaining to my parents. This freaked my mom out. It wasn't just because of the impropriety of having Richard in the house—our family had lots of skeletons in the closet that she would rather keep hidden.

My mom started pressuring my dad to nudge Richard out of the house. He eventually caved and sat Richard down for a talk about next steps.

"This isn't a permanent solution," my dad said. "You can't stay here forever."

"Fine. I'll just go kill myself," Richard said.

He stormed out of the house and didn't come back for several days.

I was furious with my parents. If Richard had killed himself, his blood was on their hands. I swore I would never forgive them.

Of course, Richard didn't actually follow through with his threat. He slummed it in his car for a few days before showing up tired, hungry, and in need of a shower.

My parents apologized and promised not to push Richard out. I would be graduating in a year anyway, and then we could get a place of our own.

Though relieved to know that Richard was safe, I felt sick at the idea of living alone with him. I was feeling more and more trapped by the day. It was clear that everyone just assumed we would get married.

DON'T ASK, DON'T TELL

If Richard was going to be staying in the house, my parents didn't want us having sex. My mom would rather have died than broach the subject with me, since having a sex talk cut too close to what she had allowed to happen to me as a child. She had my dad confront me instead. She badgered him into making sure I wasn't sleeping with Richard.

My dad pulled me aside one day and told me to assure him that we weren't having sex. He naturally assumed that we already were, but he wanted my mom off his back and to be absolved of responsibility when the truth inevitably came out.

If we were going to be having sex in the house, they didn't want to *know* about it. My mother, in particular, was completely averse to confrontation. She would rather just not know about anything unpleasant or problematic. If she did know about it, she would pretend otherwise.

I did my part and denied everything. Of course we weren't having sex!

This conversation was incredibly uncomfortable for me, and I just wanted it to end. But my dad seemed to enjoy it. He still liked teasing me about sex. Although the sexual abuse had stopped, his inappropriate comments had not. He still did degrading things like holding lingerie up against my body to see who "looked best in it," me or my mom. The touching had stopped, but the inappropriate innuendo had not. When he bought a new motorcycle, he told me to put on some daisy dukes and hop on the back, saying, "I need a cute blonde on the back with me."

My dad would even talk this way in front of Richard. This was obviously uncomfortable for me given my history with my father. I would turn red and slink away as quickly as possible, pretending not to hear him.

Avoid, avoid, avoid. I was just as invested in keeping family secrets as my mom. I was as worried as she was that talking about sex would bring up what had happened to me. That was not something I wanted to think about—ever. I worried that it would tear the family apart. I was afraid one of them would die by suicide or disappear overnight. They would have every reason to do so if the truth ever came out.

Of course, as always, it was up to me and me alone to make

sure that never happened. I had to hold strong and be the glue that kept them together. I had to carry our secrets.

These were open secrets, of course. Everyone knew the truth about me and my father. Everyone knew Richard and I were sexually active. But we had to feign ignorance. We couldn't talk about these things openly, ever—not to anyone, not even to each other.

This meant that I had no one to confide in. Richard couldn't help; he was half the problem at hand. I couldn't go to my mom or dad either, obviously. I couldn't even turn to my brother. My only comfort was the basset hound my parents let me get for my eighteenth birthday.

There was nowhere to turn for support outside the house either. Our family was too different to have close family friends. I was scared to talk to anyone in the church about my secrets. There weren't even teachers or counselors I could trust. The adults at school could be just as creepy as the other men in my life. My high school principal once slapped my butt while I was bending over to retrieve a soda from the vending machine. A teacher once told me to sit in the front row of the class because he liked seeing me in skirts.

I didn't complain or think this was all that inappropriate. It was just how men were, in my mind. In fact, I indulged them. I sat up front in my skirts and positioned my legs to give the teacher a good view. None of this was in exchange for better grades or any demand on my part. It was just how I was conditioned to behave around men. I expected this behavior from them. It didn't seem like a problem. But I certainly couldn't turn to them for help.

I couldn't even turn to Sara. She took church rules so seriously, she would never permit us to maintain our friendship if she knew I was sleeping with Richard.

She once approached me about something I had said to Richard. We had been in the basement making out. He was staring at my chest and obviously wanted my shirt off. I didn't know whether I should take it off or let him.

"If you had a really good piece of candy, would you want to unwrap it or would you want me to unwrap it for you?" I had asked, trying to sound sultry.

Richard must have repeated this phrase to John, who repeated it to Sara. She wanted to know if I had really said it.

I denied everything. I lied right to her face.

Anything to keep a secret. Anything to keep *all* our secrets.

TRIAL BY RICHARD

I made the mistake of turning to Richard. I told him how terrified I was of my parents finding out that we were having sex. My greatest vulnerability was now exposed. Richard had no reservations about using it against me. He started threatening to tell everyone we had been having sex if I ever left him.

As if to show he meant business, to keep the threat active, Richard would take risks when we had sex. We sometimes had sex at the grocery store where he worked. There was a refrigerated section in the floral department where work-ers could stock the shelves from behind. He would take me in through the back and have sex with me where anyone walking by looking for flowers could have seen us.

He took risks at home too, which was even worse. When my parents were watching television in the living room, he would sometimes take me around the corner and have sex with me right there in the hallway, quietly, but all it would have taken was my parents getting up and walking out of the room.

Part of me believes they knew what was going on. How could they not? We weren't even ten feet away. At the time, though, I really believed they did not know—that they *could not* know. I couldn't let Richard tell, which meant I was completely at his mercy. Any vague notions I might have had of someday leaving him flew out the window.

His newfound leverage over me emboldened him, and he began showing his uglier side. Richard took advantage of the time my parents spent away looking at cabin properties to subject me to sexual deviancies so heinous they can only be described as abuse, especially since he would coerce me through blackmail when begging didn't work. He had me lie naked on the floor with my legs spread while he gathered things to insert inside of me. He used all kinds of household items—pencils, whisks, spatulas, screwdrivers, even the han-dle of a hammer.

This was excruciatingly painful, and he would subject me to this for what felt like hours, as his ultimate goal, he claimed, was to "stretch me out" enough to fit his fist inside of me, an idea he had gotten from pornography.

By this point, he had stopped trying to hide his pornography addiction. He used to try to hide it from me. If I walked in on him while he was looking at porn on the computer, he would close the screen so that I couldn't see. I once found a nude picture he had printed out sitting in the family printer. Richard made up some story about someone from school inserting it into the file he was printing. He called it an "auto-print." When I asked the techs at the computer store whether this was possible, they snickered and said no.

This was distressing. Porn was definitely a sin. I told Richard we were done and wouldn't let him get a word in before hanging up the phone. My father saw me crying and asked what was wrong. I fought back tears while telling him that Richard was looking at pornography.

My dad rolled his eyes. "Get the hell out of here. I can't deal with this," he said. "Come back when you're sane."

Now that Richard had leverage over me, there was no way I could threaten to leave him. When I walked in on him looking at porn, he no longer turned off the computer. He motioned me over to watch with him.

This was extremely triggering for me. Online pornography had exploded, and Richard had clearly gone down the rabbit hole and gotten hooked on some of the most extreme and vile stuff.

I couldn't handle watching it. Richard once put on *Striptease*, the notoriously racy Demi Moore movie from the nineties. Even that had been too much. We were in my room late at night, when everyone else was asleep. The sex scenes brought back images of what happened to me as a child, and I broke down and started crying uncontrollably.

Richard reached for me, but I crawled across the floor to get away from him.

"Sorry, sorry," he said. "I didn't think it would be like this."

He seemed genuinely concerned at the time, though it wasn't enough to stop him from asking me to watch porn with him.

"What happened to you?" he asked me directly one time. "Something is wrong. Tell me what happened to you."

I got the sense that he knew exactly what had happened. I could hear the truth in his voice. He knew.

This was confirmed later when I overheard him comparing notes about me with my dad. My body was something they had in common. Outrageously, my father liked to talk to Richard about abusing me. He was reliving those days vicariously through Richard.

"I bet you enjoy that ass, don't you," I once overheard my father saying from the next room. It wasn't a question.

"Yeah, it's pretty good," Richard agreed, sheepishly.

Hearing them acknowledge what had happened changed nothing for me. Nor did confirmation that my dad knew I was sleeping with Richard. You don't really *keep* open secrets. You can only suppress them. That it was acknowledged privately was no reason to make a big deal about it. Everyone knew everything.

So I carried on as before, still under Richard's thumb, his behavior becoming ever more abusive and controlling.

He was always giving me these little "tests." These were formal appraisals and trials. They sometimes focused on my body. Richard detested cellulite, which he called "cottage cheese." He would have me lie flat on the floor while he gripped my arms and thighs and twisted the flesh between his hands to check for excess body fat.

I was absolutely tiny, not even a hundred pounds wet. Still, Richard forced me to lie there while he poked and prodded at my body, his fingers impromptu calipers.

Sometimes he had me lie in his lap while he cupped my breasts with his hand. I would pass if he could get a handful. This test worried me far more; I was rail-thin and flat-chested. But he always let me pass, as these tests were less about my body than my willingness to submit to his indignities. The size and shape of my body were known quantities. It was my unconditional loyalty that was really being tested.

Lucky me, if there was one thing I knew, it was how to submit to the unreasonable demands of men. I passed every time.

These tests became increasingly more extreme. Richard sometimes tested my loyalty by leaving me alone in strange places. He once left me alone on a park bench for hours. I wasn't supposed to wander off or talk to anyone. I couldn't move an inch until he came back.

"If you really love me," he said, "you'll still be here."

I watched him walk away.

Hours passed. The sun went down. I was alone in the dark. This was absolutely terrifying for me. I kept looking over my shoulder and scanning the shadows. Every small noise made me jump.

As the hours ticked by, I worried he wouldn't come back at all. Even though this would have dramatically improved my life, this was a terrifying prospect at the same time. I may not have liked him, but his approval meant everything to me. I judged myself by his standards now. How he saw me was how I saw myself. I had to pass these tests. I needed his validation.

This was not dissimilar to how I had felt about my father. I had never wanted my father to show me any sexual attention, but it felt like my fault that he had stopped, as if I had done something wrong. I didn't want Richard to abandon me any more than my father had, even though they were my abusers. My mindset was unfathomable to anyone who has never suffered this kind of abuse.

I did not like them. I did not like what they were doing to me. However, they set the rules, and my job was to listen and follow. So if Richard had a test for me, no matter how seemingly arbitrary or deranged, of course I needed to pass it.

My fear of abandonment, beginning with this episode, persisted for a long time afterward. It was the same fear I later experienced when Eric, my trafficker, left me with strange men. I was terrified that he wouldn't return, and I felt profound relief whenever he, my sex trafficker, did come back to collect me for future abuse.

So, too, I was relieved to finally see Richard emerge from the dark, cutting across the park, coming to collect me.

WHAT THEY DIDN'T KNOW...
WHAT THEY DID

The question of how much my parents knew about what was going on is an open one. They seemed so oblivious as to be willfully in the dark. My parents weren't dumb—but they sure put on a good act at being completely clueless about my life. So much of it was right out in the open, and I don't just mean the risks Richard was taking by having sex with me practically in plain sight.

When I was eighteen, my mom took me to see a gynecologist for the first time. She told me this was the proper age to start going, which isn't accurate, given that every professional gynecological institution in the country recommends girls see a gynecologist for the first time when they are between thirteen and fifteen. Clearly, my mom didn't care that much about my sexual health, but she cared plenty about my sexual history, or so it seemed.

Her ulterior motive, which she took no pains to hide, was that she wanted the gynecologist to confirm that I was a virgin—or, more precisely, that I was *not*.

I wish she would have been more discreet about her intentions, as Richard heard her talking about taking me. He demanded to come along. My mom told him no and that it was between a mother and daughter, a private matter. Besides, Richard was just my boyfriend, and it wouldn't have been proper.

Richard wouldn't back down. Rather than trying to persuade my mom, he worked on me instead. He demanded to come along and wouldn't leave me alone until I asked my mom to let him join us. She resisted, but I insisted on his behalf, even though it was odd to have my boyfriend coming to my first gynecology appointment.

Richard waited in the lobby with her when I was called back. For some reason, my mom took me to see a male gynecologist rather than a woman. The entire experience was terribly traumatizing, as it dredged up memories of being abused as a child. I don't think this was intentional on her part since she was in denial about what happened to me as a child. Regardless, I came out of the exam room sobbing.

Richard rushed over and put his arm around me, trying to console me, and surprisingly I was glad to have him there. My mother looked at me with disgust, presuming the exam had revealed her assumption to be true. She kept asking what had happened and why I was so upset.

I couldn't even answer; I was crying too hard to talk. When I finally could get a word out, all I would say was that everything was fine.

In fact, the doctor hadn't said anything about whether or not I was a virgin. He hadn't even brought it up, although my mom had made it seem as if that was the whole point of the visit. I had been very nervous about the appointment as a result, thinking the gynecologist would take one look at me and then declare to my family and all the world that I had been having sex with my boyfriend.

She wouldn't let it go, but I wouldn't say anything other than that I was fine, never mind the tears streaming down my face. She tried to get the doctor to talk to her, but I was eighteen and HIPAA prevented him from telling her anything, thank God.

My mom was angry the whole ride home. In addition to being upset that no one could confirm what she thought she already knew, it offended her deeply that Richard was consoling me when she hadn't even wanted him there to begin with.

Though it wasn't as if she was even trying to console me, it upset her that someone else was doing what she should have been doing. I don't think she even wanted to console me; she just hated to see someone else make her look bad.

Why did she take me in the first place? Given what happened to me as a child, it is surprising that she would want to press the matter of my virginity, especially so openly. Perhaps the abuse was, in fact, why she was so focused on proving that I had been sleeping with Richard.

She really seemed to think that the doctor was going to come out and reveal my tainted status right in front of her. I think she wanted something to lord over me, to say, "Look, you lied, and I caught you." But I also think she wanted to prove, for all to see, that the reason I was not a virgin was because I had been having sex with my boyfriend.

Because if I was *not* a virgin and also *not* having sex with my boyfriend, well, then who exactly had been having sex with me?

SIX

AN "HONEST WOMAN"

Before long, there was simply no question as to whether or not Richard and I would get married. It was just assumed that we would.

Richard was always dropping hints about our future together. He would say things like, "One of these days, I'll make an honest woman out of you."

This wasn't just rhetoric—he was more or less serious. Getting married young wasn't unusual in the LDS community but living together out of wedlock definitely was.

Did I like Richard? No.

Did I want to marry him? Yes.

It really was the only way to make an "honest woman" of me, as far as I could see. We were already having sex, which was, again, the greatest violation of church doctrine. Marriage was the only acceptable solution to the sinful choices we had already made, along with those I was still making at the time by giving in to Richard's sexual advances and blackmail. There was no other way to absolve myself of these sins and move on with my life, so I would simply have to lean into them instead.

This prospect made me anxious but marrying Richard would be a huge relief. It would mean one less family secret to hide, as sex in marriage is expected of you. Of course, sex had basically *always* been expected of me specifically, but marriage would in this case mean no more hiding and lying.

I was so resigned to a life with Richard, and the decision felt so completely out of my hands anyway, that it was easy to look for silver linings. What did it matter? Richard was the man who had chosen me, so of course we would marry, and since this was the case, I might as well look forward to the day with anticipation.

And so I did—I looked forward to marrying a man whom I didn't want to marry.

Marriage is supposed to be a happy thing, right? So any doubts about *this* particular marriage were rendered moot by the inevitability of it all.

AN INDECENT PROPOSAL

When Richard finally proposed, I was still eighteen, only a year out of high school. He popped the question during a trip to Seattle. We had always wanted to visit Seattle, fascinated as we were by the grunge and alternative music scenes rooted there at the time. We were obsessed with bands like Nirvana and Pearl Jam and the entire mythology of the city.

My parents would never have let me go on an out-of-state trip without them before, but, technically an adult now, I was allowed a slightly longer leash. They said we could go to Seattle *for the day.*

We promised to fly into the city in the morning and back out that same night. This was a lie right from the start, which surely they knew—who flies across state lines for an afternoon outing?—but they had our promise, so it wasn't on them for letting us spend the night together unsupervised.

We called them from Seattle that evening to say we were stuck in the airport and wouldn't make it home until the next day. My parents bought the lie, or at least they pretended to believe it. They could have easily called the airport to get the flight information, but they either didn't bother or didn't tell us. It was just *okay*, no questions asked—their usual approach when there was something they didn't want to confront directly.

Richard took me to a restaurant in the Space Needle. I suspected his plans before we even left the hotel. The two of us getting all dressed up for a fancy dinner? No, that was not our relationship, not my Richard. He was not a romantic guy. He was the kind of person to scoff at restaurants with dress codes and "overpriced" menus. He thought all of it was pretentious. He would normally never take me to such a place, especially as part of a romantic date.

I mean, this was a guy who still wouldn't kiss or hold hands in public. No way would he normally be caught dead doing something so romantic, so it was a giveaway right from the start. This was no normal date; I knew what he had planned before he even started rummaging through his things for the ring.

Richard was characteristically understated in his proposal. *Proposal* is a good word for it, as he didn't actually *ask* for my hand in marriage so much as set the ring before me on the table.

"Here it is," he said, pointing at the ring, not saying much else.

I jumped out of the booth and went around to the other side to hug him.

Seemingly embarrassed, Richard recoiled a little and shooed me away. "Come on, don't make a scene."

Now *this* was the Richard I knew. He was practically pulling at his own collar, chafing against the clothes and the ambience and the notion of getting engaged. He was too cool to have anyone see him get excited about anything, even his own engagement.

This should have all been off-putting, enough to make a girl say no, but I was genuinely overcome with emotion and giddy with excitement. This was my chance to stop being a *bad girl*— nothing could ruin that for me. Being a devoted wife meant not being a promiscuous, sinful girl. Finally, finally, he was leading me out of that purgatory and into a respectable life. It really was such a relief, all things considered.

There were obvious reasons to be worried, given this was Richard, but in my head, marriage was a total game changer that would magically fix everything. Richard would start treating me right, we would have a family, everything would be better.

The pornography stuff would stop, as we would be husband and wife, so it had to—right? There was no place for stuff like that in a marriage.

Right?

In fact, everything would *not* become better, and nothing would change. Richard made this abundantly clear that very night. When we got back to the hotel, he brought out a gift "for me," which was clearly a gift for himself. He had bought me lingerie, some trashy leather body harness that looked straight out of his pornography videos. It was one part cheesy, one part tawdry, entirely revolting. It was literally crotchless. I was already making plans to "forget" it at the hotel; I didn't want to bring it home and have my parents find it.

I faked enthusiasm and appreciation and tried to put it away, but he got out his Polaroid camera so that I could pose for photos. This made me feel incredibly cheap and tacky, as cheap and tacky as the harness. All I could think was *this is really what you had in mind after proposing?*

I tried to keep up a good attitude and not let this kill the mood. Stiff upper lip, always.

We stayed the night in the hotel and flew back the next day. I told my parents we were engaged and that was that.

YOU WERE WARNED

I planned the wedding together with my mom. We did absolutely everything on our own. We found the venue, planned the itinerary, ordered everything, did everything—and I mean literally everything. We sent out invitations for both sides of the aisle. Richard didn't do anything except pick out his tux.

My family also paid for everything since Richard was still not on speaking terms with his mom and stepdad. This gave my parents leverage over how things were going to go. My mom insisted that we invite Richard's mom, Cathy, to the wedding.

Why? Richard and I both wondered.

We didn't want her there. We thought she was absolutely horrible—or, rather, Richard thought she was horrible, so of course I agreed.

My mom said inviting her was the right thing to do, which really meant that she thought it was the *appropriate* thing to do. It might appear unseemly not to invite the mother of the groom. She was, as always, all about keeping up appearances. She added Cathy to the guest list and forced me to send her an invitation.

This must have been the first Cathy heard about the wedding. She showed up at the house unannounced one day while Richard and I were sitting out in the front yard. She parked her minivan right in the middle of the street and started pounding the horn.

My mom came running out of the house to see what the commotion was all about. She saw us frozen in the yard and Cathy laying on the horn with all she had.

Cathy stuck her head out the window and started shouting, "Don't you let your daughter marry him. He's a monster. He's going to destroy her life!"

Richard took a step toward the van, but Cathy rolled the window back up and took off before he could say a word.

My mom later pulled me aside while everyone else was out of the house. It was still a few months out from the wedding.

"I got a letter from Cathy," she said.

She wouldn't let me actually see the letter, which she said was quite nasty, but she wanted me to know about it. Cathy had written a long screed denouncing her own son. She made Richard out to be a truly horrible person hiding beneath a thin veneer of normality. She described hidden sexual deviancies that he had needed serious treatment to address.

My mom wasn't buying any of these things about Richard, whom she still adored more than her own daughter. She wouldn't believe a word of the accusations Cathy made. She said we already knew the real Richard, and the real Richard wasn't some monster.

I didn't want to believe it either. I say *want* because the warning signs were so obvious that denial was the only thing keeping me from owning up to the truth about my fiancé. I didn't have to trust Cathy about what she said he was hiding; Richard had shown me his true colors already, his capacity for being nasty, cruel, and perverse. All I had to do was open my eyes and see it. I didn't want it to be true, so, as usual, I pretended that it was not. It was too hard to accept, so I just didn't. I chose not to see, just like my mom, probably the same way she had refused to see what my father was capable of.

Cathy wasn't a perfect mother, and I don't mean to imply otherwise, but she was right about her son. She was his mother, who had raised him since he was a baby, so of course she knew the real Richard better than we did. I should have listened when she tried to warn us.

THE BEST DAY OF THE *REST* OF YOUR LIFE

The letter and all the horrible things Cathy had to say about her son weren't enough to dissuade my mom from inviting her to the wedding. My parents were adamant that she be allowed to come.

So come she did...and how!

Cathy sulked and brooded throughout the entire ceremony and reception. She wouldn't smile for any of the pictures. She wouldn't talk to anyone, not at length. Not that anyone wanted to talk to her, as she was such a downer that everyone shied away from her. The whole thing was incredibly awkward, and she basically ruined the wedding as far as I was concerned. I took this as proof that Richard was right—she was a horrible person after all, and there was no reason to believe her "lies."

Cathy aside, the wedding was mostly unremarkable. The ceremony was standard; the reception was alcohol free given that we were nominally Mormon, so there wasn't much revelry or anything of the sort. The wedding was small and sparsely attended, even by small-town standards. Richard and I didn't really have friends by this point. He didn't want me to have friends, not even platonic girlfriends, which is why Sara didn't even come. We had already lost contact.

Richard didn't even like me having close friends in the family. He used to harass me about a cousin with whom I was close, which he didn't like; it looked too much like friendship. Two women spending time together meant they were lesbians, he used to tell me. Whenever I saw my cousin, he would drill me with absolutely insane questions. What had we been doing? Did we get naked together? Had we kissed?

His questions made me extremely uncomfortable. This was literally my cousin! I told him it wasn't like that, don't be crazy, but he wouldn't listen. This got so troublesome that I eventually just stopped seeing my cousin. Going out with anyone wasn't worth his harassment, so I just didn't, which made it impossible to make or keep friends.

Most of the people at the wedding I barely knew. People from the church came, but they weren't really friends, not mine, and not really even my parents'. They only came because my parents sometimes attended church, if irregularly. I didn't mind them being there, but they meant little to me. Their presence thrilled my mother, as it gave the impression that we were a normal family with friends and community ties.

We were not a normal family, though, and this was not a normal wedding. Richard acted weird the whole time. He didn't want to do anything that was expected of him as the groom. He wouldn't kiss me or hold hands. He didn't even want to stand next to me for wedding pictures and acted resentful when he had to do so.

I was accustomed to him giving me the cold shoulder for no reason but never expected him to do it on our wedding day. He barely talked to me. It was like he was shunning me on our wedding day.

People noticed. They asked why we weren't even holding hands.

"He thinks it's cliché," I had to explain, trying to play it cool as if it wasn't embarrassing.

I made excuses for him, but it was confusing and hurtful. This all made me feel really alone. It was like he was intentionally *trying* to ruin the wedding.

A limo was supposed to whisk us away at the end of the reception. It was really important to me that we leave together all dressed up. I had built it up as this symbolic expression of us moving on to our new lives together.

Richard quickly disavowed me of such a silly notion. Shortly before the limo arrived, he came down after having changed into shorts and a tank top. I was still in the gown my mom had helped me pick out from the department store. It wasn't anything fancy, but it was nice and looked good on me. When I saw him dressed like that, with me still in my wedding dress, I couldn't take it anymore. Tears filled my eyes.

"Why did you do that?" I asked. "I'm still in my dress. We were going to leave in our outfits, I thought."

"I'm just not going to do that," he said.

This was intended to wreck my day, no ifs, ands, or buts about it. He was clearly trying to upset me by ruining something important to me. It would have cost him nothing to keep his suit on, and the only reason he got changed was because he knew it would hurt me.

He climbed into the limo in those denim shorts and a wife-beater, with me following in my dress while trying to wipe tears and smudged mascara from my face. Richard started talking about the radio and other swank features of the limo. I started bawling again.

"What's wrong with you?" he asked, disgusted.

"I just thought it would be romantic. I thought it would be about us," I said. "Like, this is not how I pictured my wedding."

He shrugged. "Well, I'm sorry to let you down. This is just life."

He kept fiddling with the radio the whole way back to the hotel. He still wouldn't hold my hand, wouldn't kiss me, wouldn't so much as look at me. He gave me the silent treatment the entire way. It was horrible, and I literally wanted to die.

Back at the hotel, it was more of the same. Rather than carry me across the threshold, Richard pointed into our room and said, "Come on, get in."

We dropped our bags inside. Richard plopped down on the bed with the remote and started flipping through television stations. I stood there in my wedding gown not knowing what to do. I had expected him to lead me to the bed and slowly undress me. When that didn't happen, and it was abundantly clear that it wouldn't, I went to the bathroom and changed into pajamas.

Richard ignored me for hours while I sat crying by myself. We were only a few hours into married life, and I was already overcome with remorse and regret. I had barely slipped out of my wedding gown, but I already wanted a divorce.

When Richard finally decided to pay me any attention, it was to give me more lingerie. This was not the kind of attention I wanted. There was nothing romantic about it whatsoever. He was playing dress-up with me and parading me around the hotel room on our wedding night. It made me feel cheap and used, just like the night we got engaged. Again, I tried to be a good sport but couldn't keep myself from crying, and he blamed *me* for ruining the day.

THE HONEYMOONERS

The next morning, Richard's uncle showed up at the hotel to give us a ride to the airport. We were going on a honeymoon in Seattle. Richard invited him into the room. Hesitant, his uncle was clearly uncomfortable, but Richard waved him in.

I was still getting ready and dressed. The whole thing was terribly awkward. My eyes were red and swollen from crying, but Richard pretended like nothing had happened—no fighting, no night of me sobbing quietly in the bathroom. He didn't even acknowledge the fact that he had just gotten married! It was just like any other day, nothing special. He sat there watching TV with his uncle while I packed my things and got ready to go.

The honeymoon was no better. We spent a few days "together" in Seattle, but I might as well have gone alone. Richard gave me the same standoffish treatment from arrival until departure. He didn't want to talk about anything, especially not the wedding.

He got angry when the hotel concierge greeted us as "the honeymooners." Richard looked around sheepishly, not wanting to acknowledge the fact, as he thought honeymoons were cliché and lame. This was just our first trip together as a married couple, a few days in Seattle, nothing to get worked up about.

These were dark days, the first days of my marriage. I realized right away how big of a mistake getting married had been, but there was nothing to be done about it now. It hung over my head like a dark cloud the entire trip, making the city seem surreal. I felt ghostlike, like a wraith moving through the streets, haunting my own hotel room.

My mental health was not good. I couldn't believe how stupid I had been. I really thought things were going to be different once we were married. I thought *he* was going to be different.

But Richard wasn't different. Richard was Richard. The only thing that had changed was that I was now bound to him legally by the full power of the law. It was nothing but self-delusion that had made me believe it could ever be otherwise, and it was my own passivity that now kept me from doing anything to get away.

I was kicking myself. It wasn't like I was dumb. Deep down inside, I had known this was how things would be. Getting married just felt like the only way to get out of the situation I was in, but if I had felt trapped before, it was doubly so now. The inevitability of marrying Richard had become the reality, which was far, far worse.

It was a mistake for which I would soon pay dearly.

SEVEN

THE NEWLYWEDS

xactly as everyone had predicted, Richard and I ended up getting married. Nothing had changed for me; I still felt as if my life wasn't truly my own. Decisions were being made that I had no real choice in, no option but to comply with. If Richard wanted to get married, that would be my fate.

Shortly before our marriage, Richard and I bought a little mobile home not far from where we had lived with my parents. Richard moved in before the wedding, and I joined him when we got back from our honeymoon in Seattle.

We lived in that trailer for five years, through the end of the nineties and into the new millennium—and I absolutely hated the place. The trailer was falling apart and infested so badly that I often stayed the night at my parents' house just to get away from the mice. They were everywhere. You could hear them skittering in the walls and beneath the floors, all day and all night long.

None of this seemed to bother Richard, who didn't mind living in a dump so long as the price was right.

What was the price? I didn't really know, not exactly. Richard controlled our finances, and I wasn't allowed knowledge of the fine details, as it wasn't my place. Richard had total control over and final say on all our finances, our entire lives.

He made all the decisions about everything all the time—what we did, what we ate, where we lived—so, in his mind, why did I need to know about our finances? Finances were irrelevant to my role as procurer of groceries and household goods.

If Richard's role in our marriage was the executive, mine was clearly the secretary. I was given an allowance of ten dollars cash each week to spend however I liked. Everything else, which included all of our groceries and household items, went on a debit card. Every Saturday morning, we sat down at the kitchen table to go over what was on the card that week. I had to produce receipts for everything so that Richard could scrutinize every single purchase.

"Why did you buy a mousetrap?" (Because we have mice?)

"You spent *this much* on bread?" (Well, the pantry was empty.)

These sessions always ended with him finding something to be mad about. No matter how unremarkable and routine my purchases, Richard would go on a rampage about some "unnecessary" expense, such as laundry detergent or new socks, the real *luxuries* of life. Without fail, he would always accuse me of being irresponsible with money and threaten to take the debit card away.

Of course, he never actually took the card away, as it wasn't as if he was going to do the shopping himself. He just had to go through this same song and dance every weekend to keep me on my toes and in my place. I just had to sit there and listen to him yell for an hour or two before he would finally give me "one last chance" with the card.

Given this dynamic, one might assume Richard was the breadwinner and I the stay-at-home homemaker—but I was not. We both worked.

After high school, I took a course in travel and tourism with the intent to become a travel agent. This was a bad fit for me, so I decided to switch to beauty school, but I didn't like that either. After dropping out of beauty school, I settled into an administrative support position with a dog breeders' association and continued working similar jobs thereafter.

But my money wasn't my own—our money was *his*. Throughout our marriage, my paychecks went straight into a "joint" account that I had no access to or control over. Only Richard could access the account.

Richard paid bills while I sat dutifully at his side, watching him make out the checks. His running commentary during these sessions wasn't so different from our weekly review of household expenses.

Richard would huff and puff as he wrote each check. The only time he displayed dissatisfaction with the trailer or our lot in life was when it came time to pay. Then "all we could afford," which he usually called a good deal, was suddenly a rip-off.

"Look how much we pay for this."

"Goddamn, this is so expensive. Can you believe we pay that?"

"We're never going to get out of this trailer. We are going to live here forever. If we pay this much for a trailer, imagine what a *house* costs."

I just nodded along, trying to keep him from getting riled up. *No, honey, I can't believe what the internet costs.*

Occasionally, Richard would ask whether I wanted to fill out a check myself, as if this were some kind of honor or special treat. Never mind that I didn't have any actual say over how our money—including my own paychecks—was spent. I was just supposed to be happy to pick up the pen once in a while to sign a check, as if I were cutting the ribbon at some big ceremony.

THE MARRIAGE CONTRACTS

As tight as money supposedly was, Richard always seemed to find money for whatever he really wanted.

Case in point: his white '77 Corvette.

Shortly before getting married, we went to an auto show together, which wasn't something he just dragged me along to, as I was just as enthusiastic about cars as he was, maybe even more so. This is where we spotted the Corvette. Richard fell head over heels for it—faster and harder than he ever had for me.

There was no six-month courtship to speak of here; this was love at first sight. Richard practically salivated all over that car.

Of course, we didn't have the money for a car like that just sitting around in a bank account. However, our financial reality wasn't enough to deter Richard, who wanted me to sell *my* car to put the money toward the Corvette.

This seemed like a really bad idea, but Richard really sold me on the car—*our* car, as he spoke of it at the time. He told me to think about taking the Corvette out on the highway with the top down and the wind in our hair. We could take turns taking it to work. We could take the Corvette out for ice cream and up the hill to look down on the town at night.

My car wasn't exactly mine to sell, though, as my parents had helped me pay for all my vehicles, which had always bugged Richard. When we met, I was driving an old red car my parents bought for my sixteenth birthday, nothing special, but it was my first car. Coming home from school to find this red car sitting in the driveway had sent me into ecstatic glee.

Eventually, I sold the red car for a Land Cruiser, which Richard was completely jealous of. He called me a spoiled brat, and he absolutely flipped his lid when my parents helped me trade the Land Cruiser toward a newer car one of my mom's friends was selling. We got a good deal on the new car, but the money from the Land Cruiser wasn't enough for an even trade, so my parents paid the difference.

This made Richard absolutely furious. He *hated* seeing me in that car. Richard drove us everywhere, as he straight refused to ride in something I "didn't deserve." He couldn't even be near me when the car was around; he couldn't stand to see it in the driveway.

None of this made sense to me. For one, he was driving a Corvair at the time, which was also one of his dream cars, so he had nothing to be jealous of. My new car was a stick and really zipped, but it was nothing fancy.

Moreover, we were boyfriend and girlfriend. We were getting married. Why couldn't he be happy for me? Why did my having something nice upset him so much?

After we got married, one of the first things Richard did was make me sell that car. I traded down for something less nice that he thought was more befitting of me—and now he wanted me to sell *that* car too!

When I mentioned selling my car to put the money toward the Corvette, my parents said absolutely not—it wasn't happening. The car was my ride to and from work, and it didn't make sense to be sharing a car with Richard when we were both working.

Although I knew this would upset Richard, I was relieved that my parents stuck up for me for once. They seemed to intuit that the Corvette wouldn't really be mine to share, and since this was a matter of me getting myself to work, they put their foot down. Maybe they just didn't want to end up having to help me get another car, but this was one of the few times they took a stand on my behalf when Richard was pushing me around.

Richard ended up buying the Corvette anyway, probably by taking out a loan from his uncle. I wasn't really sure where exactly he got the money since he allowed me so little insight into our financial decisions. He might well have taken money from our "joint" bank account, as I had no way of knowing for sure.

So this is how it happened that we had a fancy sports car sitting in front of our rundown trailer. Richard cherished that car so much that he was scared to take it out on the road. He normally took the Corvair to work and left the Corvette sitting in the driveway, as if it were his manhood sitting and gleaming out front.

Of course, I was not allowed to touch the Corvette. When I asked Richard when I could take it out for a spin, he answered, "Never. You are not going to drive it."

"Are you serious? You are not going to let me drive it even once?"

Richard told me that I would need to fill out an application in order to drive the car. This might sound shocking to most people: *Your husband made you fill out an application to drive his car? Who does that?* My husband did that, and it seemed more or less normal for our marriage. I was already conditioned to Richard and his little "tests," so a formal test or an application was really not that different from how he had forced me to sit in his lap while he assessed my excess body fat, or how he had made me prove my loyalty by waiting alone in the park at night for his return. After suffering through all of that, a formal test was a piece of cake.

Richard typed up the application on the computer and printed it out to look all formal. I filled it out by hand. This was no simple multiple-choice quiz. The application was several pages long and included large spaces for me to write in my answers in paragraph form. The test quizzed me on traffic laws and automotive maintenance. Some of the questions were basic driver's ed questions, probably ripped from actual tests, but others delved so deep into the esoteric workings of sports car engines and other automotive minutiae that it was clear he had done research online just to stump me.

Other questions were intended to send a message, such as those asking how much the car cost, belaboring the point—as if I wasn't well aware of what the Corvette was worth. I knew what it was worth: more than we could afford, I wanted to write. If we *were* going to have the damn thing, I might as well be able to drive it too sometimes, so I gave the answers he wanted to hear and handed the application back to Richard.

He reviewed my answers and later called me over to go over my application. It should come as no surprise that he failed me unceremoniously, never mind that I was arguably a better driver than him. It didn't matter, as he was the one administering the test, and my answers hadn't ever mattered anyway. There was no way he was ever going to pass me because he didn't want me driving the car. The test was just a big production to give him an excuse to prohibit me from ever driving the Corvette.

There were no redos, so I couldn't retake the test. That was that: the car was his and his alone.

This didn't keep Richard from going on and on about the car. He was always bragging about how well it handled and how other women supposedly looked at him admiringly on the highway. What he *didn't* talk about was taking me out for a ride. All the stories about taking it out on the highway to feel the wind in our hair had dried up. His promises to use the car to take me out for ice cream or up the hill to look out on the city lights had never materialized.

I asked him when we were going to take the car on some out-ings together.

"You didn't pass the driving test," he replied.

"You can drive. I just mean when are you going to take me out in it?"

This is when he informed me that I would need to fill out a separate application just to be a passenger.

"You have to be kidding me," I said, naively.

I really thought he had to be kidding me this time. A driving test, okay, but a passenger test? Was he going to quiz me on how to buckle my seat belt?

But, of course, Richard was dead serious. This really hurt, as the car was our first big purchase as husband and wife, and now he seemed dead set on cutting me out of it entirely. It wasn't *our* car at all, and likely never was in his mind; it was just his.

This is probably the moment when a stronger, less dam-aged person would have stuck up for themselves, but not me. I didn't see any way of pushing back against him, or any man for that matter. I complained just enough to make my displeasure known, but never enough to challenge him, never enough to cause a fight. I was far too worried about setting Richard off, as I was already scared of him.

As my lifelong conditioning dictated, I played by the rules set out for me. I told him to give me the application.

A couple of days later, he presented me with the second application. This one was much shorter. He passed me this time around, which was a relief, as it wasn't like there was anything wrong with my answers last time. It would have been truly embarrassing not to be able to even ride in my husband's car.

Although he may have officially conferred passenger benefits upon me, in practice he almost never let me ride along anyway. I probably rode in that car three times in all the years we had it.

TRAPPED

What I learned in that first year of marriage was that Richard was never going to change. The bright red warning signs of an abusive, controlling person that I had noted from the beginning were not going to go away.

In fact, his behavior became increasingly worse the longer we were together. He didn't become less mean—he became more so. He didn't give up pornography—he doubled down on it. He didn't start to cherish me as his wife—he clamped down harder and harder in his efforts to control me.

The longer we were together, the more he let his true colors show. If he had ever had any reservations about treating me poorly before, they were now as gone as gone could be. I had been relieved when Richard could no longer blackmail me with threats of telling my parents and the community that we were having premarital sex, but now that we were legally bound together, he had even more leverage over me. Divorce was no more socially acceptable in the community than premarital sex.

All in all, Richard had free rein to treat me as poorly as he wanted. He was always complaining about me and everything I did, everything I *was*. The ridicule never stopped. My appearance was a constant object of critique. I was too fat, my nose too big. My bottom lip stuck out too far. My profile was too masculine. And it wasn't just how I looked. He casually criticized my personality and my intelligence, making me feel stupid and intensifying my insecurity.

Everything about me was wrong, wrong, wrong.

There was no escaping this criticism because there was no escaping Richard. He accompanied me everywhere, literally. He once followed me to an event organized by a church group. I was in beauty school at the time, and they had invited me to give a demonstration for the girls. Richard came along, of course, because he wouldn't let me go anywhere without him. I was surprised they even let him in, given that it was an event for young girls, but they did. The whole way home, Richard wouldn't shut up about how badly I had blown the presentation.

None of this was true. The church loved my presentation and had told me so.

Nor was anything wrong with my body or appearance. I was absolutely tiny, so it was bizarre for Richard to always describe me as "a whole lot of woman." That is, until he would follow it up by saying that it was "a whole lot of work loving all of me."

The point of this constant criticism was to position himself as the benevolent savior figure, the only one who could ever love me, the only one who would ever even tolerate me.

Over time I started believing him. Hearing how terrible you are over and over warps your sense of self so badly that it doesn't matter how absurd the criticism has become. Your self-esteem simply cannot handle constant assault, especially once you have been isolated and rendered dependent upon your abuser.

The things Richard said about me used to hurt because he was saying them. Over time, they started to hurt because I had come to believe them.

I really thought myself incapable of being loved by anyone else. I was therefore terrified of Richard abandoning me. As horrible and cruel as he might have been, I became convinced that I was lucky to have him, or, rather, lucky that *he* would have *me*. Maybe his prospects weren't as great as he pretended, but surely neither were mine if we were together.

This is how abusers effectively manipulate their victims. They lock you away and then convince you—desperate and broken—to guard the key for them. They convince you that you have no choice but to maintain the status quo.

EIGHT

MARRIED...WITHOUT CHILDREN

My marriage, right from the beginning, was a desperately lonely time for me. Richard, when he wasn't being mean, mostly ignored me. I felt like a minor character in the story of his life, something in the background that just happened to be there, the bad wallpaper or crack in the flooring that you no longer noticed.

We were rarely ever even in the same room, as he was always on the computer playing video games, mostly flight simulators. His big dream in life was to become a pilot, but since he hadn't gone into the military and had no way of logging hours in a real cockpit, flight simulators were all he had to scratch that itch. That man lived on his computer, and so I, for all intents and purposes, lived alone in a trailer while he was off in the other room.

There was a night shortly after returning from our honeymoon, with Richard already asleep in the other room, when I sat up alone in the living room, sobbing all night long. The terrible mistake of getting married bore down on me, absolutely crushing me under its weight. I could see my whole life flattened out in front of me, stretching out forever, just Richard and me, alone in that trailer.

There was no way out, no matter how desperately I wanted out. Getting a divorce was out of the question. Getting married only to turn right around and get divorced? My parents would never speak to me again after having paid for the wedding and inviting people from church.

It didn't matter, though, as I would never actually file for divorce. I was too scared of upsetting them and Richard both. The whole thing was embarrassing. Yes, it was a huge mistake, but not one that I wanted to admit to anyone else—it was hard enough to admit it to myself.

There was also no one to talk to about any of this, which made it difficult for me to ascertain just how abusive the relationship really was. I understood that our relationship wasn't typical, but I was so conditioned to mistreatment from men that it still seemed relatively normal, even as Richard became increasingly controlling. My view of things was warped by a lifetime of abuse, and I had no one to offer an outsider's perspective. My life was already completely devoid of friends, as the wedding had demonstrated with the negligible number of my peers who attended. I hadn't seen Sara once since high school, as Richard wouldn't have me hanging out with "lesbians"—because why else would two women spend time together unless they were gay? There weren't other friends to speak of, and I had even grown distant from my cousin. Richard was the only person in my life not related by blood, and that was just how he wanted it.

My parents weren't an option either, even though they were always around. They lived right down the street, as they had sold their home and moved to be near us. This was a pattern that would continue until our ultimate falling out many years later. They uprooted and moved twice just to be closer to Richard and me.

This seemed understandable at the time, even though they never moved to be closer to my brother until many years later, after I broke off all contact with them. My suspicion now is that they were trying to keep the family secret from getting out. Keep your friends close but your liabilities closer. They were a part of my daily life, which made it even harder to talk about what had happened to me as a child.

At the time, though, newly married and living in the trailer park, I still considered my mother my best friend. She was nearby and always around. We had lunch together almost every day, and Richard and I often had dinner with my parents.

This didn't mean that I could talk with her about anything that mattered, though, certainly not the problems I was having with Richard. She didn't want to hear about them. She didn't want to hear about any of my problems. Our relationship only operated at the surface level. We would make meals together and watch mindless television, but she would shut down if I tried to talk about my problems, even though she talked incessantly about her own. She would complain about work and occasionally my father, but I couldn't complain about my relationship with Richard. When I voiced any concern over or doubts about my marriage, she quickly changed the subject. She would start talking about the weather or asking what was on TV, as if she hadn't heard me. The message was clear: everything had to be okay, and if it wasn't, she didn't want to hear about it. Eventually, I stopped even trying to bring up how I felt about my marriage.

My mom's attitude was not new; she had behaved this way my whole life. She never wanted to hear anyone say negative things about their own lives, even though she was exceedingly negative herself. I'm certain she intuited that things were bad with Richard, but she desperately wanted our family to be normal. Of course, the secret we were carrying meant that we could never be normal, so the best she could do was sweep everything under the rug. This included the abuse I had suffered from my father, as well as any abuse I might be suffering from Richard.

In many ways, my parents seemed to value their relationship with Richard over their relationship with me. They didn't want to hear anything negative about him, so I simply couldn't bring up problems we were having without them taking his side.

While my parents loved and admired Richard, he didn't always return the admiration. He was well behaved in their presence but quick to talk about them behind their backs. As his wife, I was the recipient of this duplicity. But I had to be very careful about what I repeated, as betraying Richard's trust was a cardinal offense.

Sometimes, it could be about the smallest, most inconsequential things. For example, Richard hated my parents' dog. He wanted them to put it down.

"I wish I could give it some poison," he said one night.

I didn't think he was serious. He was just mad and blowing off steam. Even Richard wouldn't do something as cruel as that, so it wasn't something I felt I needed to warn my parents about. But I once let slip that he hated the dog while we were having dinner at their house.

"You do?" they asked him.

Richard laughed it off, saying he didn't *hate* the dog. It just kind of bothered him sometimes.

When they were in the other room, Richard gave me an icy look that told me in no uncertain terms that he wanted to feed *me* poison. It was clear I had made a huge mistake bringing it up. I tried making light of the whole thing so my parents wouldn't take it seriously.

Since we lived just down the street, we went home on foot. Richard was quiet as we left, but as soon as we were out of my parents' eyeshot, he shoved me hard and sent me tumbling into the bushes.

I came climbing out of the bushes, brushing myself off. "What was that for?"

"Don't you fucking say anything I tell you to anyone ever again."

"Okay."

"I mean it. *Anything.*"

This level of violence was shocking in a whole new way, but it wasn't just the physicality of it. Richard had never been so sharp with me before. He looked at me like he wanted to tear me apart. His rage was just as frightening as being shoved to the ground.

If I had any lingering doubts before, it was now abundantly clear that talking with my parents about Richard was out of the question. I couldn't risk them repeating anything negative I voiced about Richard if this was how he reacted to a much more innocuous slip. Basically, our entire relationship was out of bounds.

In addition to my fear of reprisal, I was too ashamed to tell people, even my own parents, about Richard's behavior. Telling anyone what he did was also admitting to putting up with his behavior, which made me look just as bad, at least in my eyes. I was a pushover, a doormat, and that wasn't something I wanted to share with the world.

Your husband makes you fill out an application to ride in the car with him? What kind of woman puts up with that sort of thing?

These were the kind of thoughts that went through my head when I mulled over my marriage with Richard, so I was always covering for him, always making excuses, always carrying secrets.

That was how it had always been. I was conditioned to pretend nothing bad was happening to me. It was in my blood, in my very DNA, to protect those who were hurting me.

A WAY OUT

Stuck in a bad marriage that was never going to get better, I became convinced only one thing could improve my life—having children.

My life was hollow, my work was fine but not something to live for, and it felt like there was no other answer to my sense of loneliness and meaninglessness. Richard was never going to let me have close friends, so children were the only answer. If I wanted another friend around, I was going to have to give birth to them. Children were the only friends he might consider letting me have.

Having children had always been a lifelong dream of mine, but overwhelming loneliness was what drove me to have kids with Richard—with the wrong person in the wrong marriage.

Some women have children to fix their relationship; I wasn't so naive as to think that anything would ever change Richard, not anymore. My hope was that kids would give me something else to focus on, something more to live for.

I wasted no time trying to convince Richard to have children. This had to be done carefully and with discretion, as Richard was not so enthusiastic about the prospect of children—not now, maybe not ever. He thought his parents had screwed him up so badly, and he didn't want to do the same thing to his own kids.

Besides, having kids was what you were supposed to do, and, per usual, Richard didn't want to conform to society's expectations of him. He said he was content with the way things were.

This was probably closer to the truth, as he was most likely simply unenthused about the notion of changing diapers and ambivalent about our marriage anyway. The way he always went on about women who were interested in him, he likely had one foot halfway out the door should anyone actually reciprocate his interest.

My strategy for changing Richard's mind about having kids was subtle. I dropped hints about wanting to start having a family of our own, how it would be nice to have more life in the house. Richard was working while going to college, and I was still considering various career paths, but with my mom so close and willing to watch the kids, there wasn't anything holding us back.

I was trying to make the case in terms that would appeal to him—he wouldn't have to do much, maybe not anything. I even tried to explain how loneliness was making me a worse wife, suggesting that motherhood would make me happier and thus a better spouse for him.

None of this seemed to work. Richard kept saying no, not now, the timing is wrong, no, no, no.

But I persisted and slowly wore him down. He eventually said that we could at least consider having a baby, but not for another three years. This seemed reasonable, as it would give him time to get through school and for us to save a little money.

Two or three years came and went. We bought our cars and worked our jobs and went to school (Richard to college and me to beauty school for a stint), and life carried on. Those years were hard and lonely, but I kept gently badgering Richard about his promise to consider having a baby, just to keep the dream alive.

When he was finally ready to consider having kids for real, not in the future, but now, he had one more stipulation for me. Just as I had been forced to fill out an application to use the Corvette, I would need to file an application with him in order to have a child. Richard said having kids was a serious matter and that he wanted to make sure we did things right. I would need to prove my commitment and worthiness and be willing to sign a formal contract defining the terms of coparenting.

By all rights, this should have ended with me laughing in his face, but I was so conditioned to this sort of thing that I was just excited for the opportunity. I didn't even think twice about having to file an application before making a major life decision instead of, you know, actually having a conversation with my husband! I recognized that these kinds of demeaning assessments weren't normal in any objective sense, so it was still embarrassing and something to conceal from outsiders, but this was *our* normal.

Besides, I was desperate for a child and would have done just about anything for one. File an application for your husband to make a determination about whether he will let you have a child? If that's the only way to have one, let me get that signed and notarized for you! Anything to have a child and cure me of my isolation and loneliness.

The application was so long that it took an hour to fill out. Again, this one required me to answer essay questions. There weren't right and wrong answers, not technically, as the right answers were just the ones Richard wanted to hear. As I answered, I had to read into the intentions behind his questions and think about what he wanted to hear.

This took time. While some of the application was just quizzing me on parenting, the meatier questions concerned how we would raise the children and, more specifically, *who* would raise them. Richard wanted to know who would change diapers and who would babysit when we went out on dates. It was very clear he expected me to handle everything and for my mom to be on call when he wanted us to get away.

Richard took several days to review the application. This was a huge decision that would shape the rest of our lives, and of course it was all his to make—there wasn't anything I could do to sway him. I feared that nagging him might sabotage the whole process, but it was impossible not to keep asking him how it was going. The suspense was killing me. It was impossible to focus on anything else, even work. My mental health suffered.

I kept asking, "Are you done yet?"

"Do you know yet?"

"Can you tell me how far along you are?"

Richard wanted me to leave him alone and trust in the process. He would simply not be rushed. Scared of upsetting him and torpedoing my own chances, I bit my tongue and let him do things on his own timeline. Everything was always on his timeline, so this was nothing new, but this was especially nerve-wracking because I had done my best on the test and there would be no second chances. It felt like my entire future hung in the balance, but I couldn't say anything for fear of upsetting him. This was my one shot at happiness.

I was terrified he would say no. I could picture it. Me and him alone in this trailer, just the two of us, forever. It was a depressing prospect, horrifying even. I imagined it stretching out for years and decades, with no way out. No way for me to change things.

Several days later, Richard came up to me nonchalantly and said that he wanted to talk about my application. My heart skipped at least three beats. He sat me down on the couch. It all felt very formal and strange, but I was chomping too hard at the bit to care. I could hardly breathe.

Richard said he had reviewed my application and wanted to let me know that I had passed.

I threw my arms around him and squeezed him tight. I was overcome with a gratitude that was completely unwarranted, that I never should have felt, and all I could do was thank him.

SIGN ON THE DOTTED LINE

My excitement aside, this wasn't a done deal just yet. Richard still wanted me to sign an official contract before I could start trying to get pregnant. Several days later, he presented me with the contract, several pages of makeshift legalese that included all kinds of terms and conditions about having a baby.

Many things that had appeared in the application showed up in the contract as well. I had to agree to be a stay-at-home mother, as he made it crystal clear that the kids would be entirely my job. This was nonnegotiable, and while no one wants to hear that their spouse isn't going to help with the kids at all, being a stay-at-home mom was what I wanted anyway. My work meant nothing to me. I also had to agree to breastfeed the children, which again was no problem, but it was bizarre that he thought it necessary to write these things into an official contract.

The one line item that gave me the most pause was a clause stipulating that I could never, ever get a divorce for any reason whatsoever, *no matter what.*

This was something Richard had often made me promise before because he thought it was a waste of his time to invest in a relationship with someone who could just leave at any point. But he was now claiming that this was about our hypothetical children, not him, as he didn't want them to suffer through a divorce.

So while his asking me to promise never to leave him wasn't new, never before had I needed to sign my name to it. Previously, I would just placate him by saying something such as, "Of course, baby, I don't want to leave you. I love you." This was how I had avoided answering the question until this point, but now I had to sign my name to his stated language. It would be there in ink, forever.

This was unnerving and ominous, but there was no other way to have a baby, so I initialed each line, signed at the bottom, and handed over the contract.

Upon receipt of the contract, Richard said okay, we could start trying to have a baby. My sense of relief and excitement was indescribable. I was twenty-three, going on twenty-four at the time. I had waited it out, I had passed Richard's tests, jumped through his hoops, the many rings of fire, and finally we were going to have a real family. A whole new world of possibility seemed open to me, having finally found a way to be happy while married to Richard, which had seemed like an utter impossibility before.

Although I will never regret having any of my kids, they were obviously not a solution to my problems. I should have realized that a prison isn't any less a prison when you share your cell with others. I was still in my cage; there would just soon be new occupants, young and innocent, living there with me as well. In my tunnel vision and desperation, I had put them there.

NINE

THERAPY WITHOUT THERAPY

After going off my birth control, I became pregnant right away. We never announced the pregnancy due to a miscarriage at six weeks, perhaps caused by all the stress I was living under.

Though what I miscarried was little more than an amorphous mass of cells, I was devastated by the miscarriage and wanted to bury the embryo. Richard wanted to throw it in the garbage can, but I insisted we drive up into the mountains to give it a proper burial. Though he was annoyed with me for taking the situation so seriously, Richard placated me by agreeing to go along.

We buried the embryo on a hillside along a trail. People were going by the freshly packed dirt while we were up there and this didn't seem right, so I decided to dig up the embryo and take it to my parents' cabin to bury it in a more isolated location. Richard still thought the whole thing was stupid, but he didn't stop me and agreed to take me up to the cabin. This was relatively nice of him, I thought, but it didn't stop him from complaining the whole way there.

THE SINGLE WIFE

Three months later, I got pregnant with my first child, Ryker. It was—surprise, surprise—not the transformative experience I had hoped for, at least not in the way I had imagined. Ryker was an angel, and I loved him dearly, but as anyone could have told me, having children only made a bad marriage worse.

Richard was a hands-off father, to say the least. It became clear, as was more or less stipulated in our contract, that Ryker was my kid and Richard's job was complete at the moment of conception. He helped out a bit with Ryker, but not much. He was working and pursuing a business degree at the University of Phoenix, so he was legitimately busy at the time, but he didn't help out any more during summers or breaks when he had more free time. He spent it on the computer or watching television instead.

By the time Asher and then Kaylee came along, Richard wasn't helping out with the kids at all. They were mine and mine alone, which he was always reminding me of as explicitly as possible.

"Get your kids to bed," he would say, not "our kids" or "those kids," but "*your* kids," thus absolving himself of any responsibility.

Not having him present as a parent was both a blessing and a curse. Richard wasn't fun to collaborate with and having him around was stressful, as he was always putting me down and making things harder.

He displayed strange hang-ups about the kids in disturbing ways. Despite having insisted in our contract on my breastfeeding, once the baby came, Richard was visibly jealous whenever I breastfed Ryker.

"Those are mine," he would say, completely serious. He directed me to stop, which was fine by me since breastfeeding was unpleasant for me. So we ended up using formula even though Richard hated having to pay for it, and he complained about the expense weekly when we went over purchases.

Richard's behavior was even stranger with Kaylee, whose diapers he was uncomfortable changing since she was a girl. This freaked me out that he would even think of her this way, for obvious reasons having to do with my own father. Whenever I had to change her I would tell him to just go, get out of the room.

Even though having Richard around more would likely have done more harm than good, raising three kids on my own was challenging. We'd moved into a house a little farther from the trailer, and there wasn't anyone around to help. My mom would occasionally help with the kids while we watched television together at her place, but at home, there was no one to help at all. The stress of raising the kids, essentially on my own, took a toll on my mind and body. I started having trouble sleeping. I felt sick all the time.

I actually came down with a bout of mono after the second baby, but when the fatigue persisted long after the infection cleared up, it became clear there was more going on. I was developing full-blown clinical depression. There were likely some postpartum issues playing a role, but the bigger issue was that my life, specifically my marriage, was horribly depressing.

Richard was a terrible father and husband, both cruel and tyrannical. Sometimes this manifested in petty behavior that made living with him a test of endurance, such as how he forced me to write a business plan every Christmas. I had to account for every penny and explain how I was getting the maximum value out of our Christmas money. There was a specific amount allotted for each member of the family, but whenever his Christmas bonus came in, he would have me apply it entirely to his share since he was "the one who earned it."

This kind of immature behavior, as low as it was, wasn't worth rocking the boat over. The boat was never worth rocking, even as his behavior got worse and worse, as his fits and rages became more extreme the longer we were together.

During the last term of my first pregnancy, Richard came home angry one day and conducted an "inspection" of the home. He scrutinized everything: the cleanliness of the floors, whether things were put away as he liked, the dust in the corners. He went through his closet, shirt by shirt, and came to one that had been hung inside out, which provided the sought-after excuse to fly into a rage.

"You're one sorry wife," he shouted. "You can't do anything right."

He tore down every shirt in his closet, and in mine as well, and tossed them on the bed before storming out of the trailer. It was left to me to clean up the mess he left behind, rehanging all the shirts and putting everything else back as it was, which wasn't easy at almost nine months pregnant and ready to burst.

The way he treated the kids wasn't much better than how he treated me. He was always calling them cruel nicknames: the little runts, the little rats, the little bastards. Sometimes, he would holler, "goodnight bitches, goodnight bastards" before retiring to bed, as if it were some big joke, but no one was laughing but him.

The kids were a new weakness that Richard could exploit, threatening me by threatening them. If Kaylee cried while he was on the computer or watching television, Richard would get really upset. He once told me, "Go shut that bitch up before I do, because you are not going to like how I do it."

These weren't idle threats. Richard seemed to derive a twisted sense of pleasure from watching the kids suffer. One time, Ryker was crying in the car because he had to go to the bathroom. Richard would not pull over and instead told Ryker that the best way to stop the feeling of having to urinate was to punch yourself in the groin as hard as you can. Ryker, an impressionable little kid, did as was suggested and punched his crotch so severely that he screamed out in pain. Richard found this hilarious and laughed for the rest of the drive home while Ryker cried in pain.

Another time, he smacked Ryker on the leg so hard that it left a handprint mark. I was always on high alert, always trying to keep the kids calm and away from him. I had to make sure they were always happy and quiet for fear of bringing his wrath down on them, which meant living constantly on edge. They were little kids, so of course they made noise and got into things. My nerves were shot trying to make sure they didn't make a peep once he got home.

Living like this was a nightmare, and while I had known kids wouldn't fix Richard, they hadn't improved my life as I had hoped they would. Everything felt even more unbearable than it had before. I loved my kids, more than the world, but they didn't make my life any more bearable. If anything, my life was harder now that I had to protect them too. This made me feel even more trapped in my marriage. Richard had never had more leverage over me than he did at that point. He even threatened to take custody of my kids if I ever tried to leave him.

I had a habit of handling emotional pain by inflicting physical pain on myself. In high school, I would cut my arms and burn the flesh with lighters, which wasn't easy to hide. When my parents spotted the burn marks, I played it off as the result of an accident with the curling iron, which they believed since I was always dropping the thing. In 2006, I started self-harming again.

Richard would never believe such an obvious lie, so I tried to avoid harming myself in a way that would attract his attention and came up with more creative forms of self-harm. I drove out into the middle of a big open field one day and put the car in park without shutting the engine off. I stripped down naked and put the air conditioner on full blast even though it was cold out. Part of me wanted to freeze to death right there in my car, which was how I always envisioned myself going out—getting colder and colder until my whole body became numb, including my mind.

Of course, this didn't work. I didn't die. I just became really, really cold.

Still, I kept on doing this when things were too much. Emotional pain was deadening, but physical pain was one of the few things that made me feel alive. The cold didn't numb me; rather, it made me feel alive. The intense cold, the pierce of a sharp edge, would snap me into the present and lift the haze hanging over me. I was walking around like a zombie most of the time and nothing else seemed to help but this, even if it was only temporary.

Punishing myself in this way was satisfying. I hated myself so much. In my mind, I *deserved* to be punished. I deserved all the pain I could inflict on myself.

YOU CAN TALK—JUST NOT ABOUT US

Although my depression was getting worse and worse throughout the marriage, I didn't seek professional help until Kaylee was about a year old. Raising three kids single-handedly had become too much, and it felt impossible to hold things together any longer on my own.

Therapy wasn't something I had ever tried before—no one in my family had because we weren't the "self-help" type—so this was completely unfamiliar, but I couldn't think of anything else that might help. It felt like a last-ditch effort to be sane.

In 2006, I told Richard that I couldn't manage things on my own anymore.

"I'm way too depressed," I said, "and starting to really scare myself."

"Come on, you're fine," he replied, batting my concerns away.

Richard could tell something was going on with me, something serious, but he expected me to be able to just snap myself out of it.

I told him, "No, I really can't."

After several weeks of begging to see a therapist, he finally agreed, but only under one condition: I was not allowed to talk about our relationship or anything that happened at home. I especially could not ever talk about him or us or our marriage. Therapy sessions had to focus on me and *only* me, as if there was some way to excise myself from my entire life.

This stipulation was basically a foregone conclusion. Richard had made it clear on multiple occasions that talking about him to anyone outside of the house was not allowed, most notably when he had knocked me into the bushes outside my parents' house. It was a point he repeated often, lest I somehow forget.

This made sense, in a way, for him. Richard had a lot to hide, after all. There was all of the abuse, of course, but also inclinations that would be embarrassing for him if they ever became public knowledge. He was even deeper into pornography than ever, which I no longer had the capacity to object to since I was dealing with so much of my own baggage. Watching porn all the time had warped his sexual interests.

His kinks became more perverse, more deviant; he had developed weird paraphilias regarding human waste. He sometimes sat by the toilet bowl, watching while I used the toilet even though it was terribly embarrassing for me. Sometimes, he asked me to undress myself and lie in the bathtub so he could urinate on me. This was all exceptionally disturbing and repellent, and he pressured me to the point where my compliance was in no way consensual.

None of this could be discussed in therapy, of course, nor the other ways he treated me, and I kept my promise both out of fear of him and embarrassment for myself. I didn't want to talk about any of that. I just wanted to feel better. Richard had convinced me that the problem was me since my life was perfect, as he put it, so there must be something broken inside of me if I could not be happy.

To a degree, I actually believed this. I had convinced myself that my relationship with Richard was more or less normal, given that he provided for me and the kids, at least monetarily. I had three beautiful children and a roof over our heads and no real concerns about money at that point, despite Richard's constant harping over every penny spent. If my life was basically normal and good, then the problem had to lie within me.

My history with my dad was a significant factor, of course, but that was buried deeper under the surface—it wasn't something I could even think about. I wouldn't let my mind venture there and couldn't talk about it either.

In other words, I couldn't talk about any of my actual problems or traumas in therapy. This meant that therapy couldn't actually be therapy.

The first thing I told my therapist was that my life was perfect, but I just couldn't be happy. There was something broken inside of me. Before going in, I had written up a ten-page report on my feelings and everything that was wrong with me, trying to explain why I couldn't be happy. I had wanted to come prepared.

My therapist looked over all ten pages but found none of it clarifying. She kept shaking her head and asking, but *why* do you feel this way?

"There must be some reason," she said. "What's going on?"

She asked this over and over, every time I came to visit. What was *really* going on here? I would just deflect the question. No, it's nothing, it's just me. This is how I am. There's no reason; I just need to be better.

Things went on this way for several months, with her drilling me for explanations and me hedging and deflecting.

This was obviously not helpful and started to feel depressing in and of itself. Having someone to talk with was nice, but we couldn't actually talk about anything that mattered. The therapist didn't know how depressed I actually was, didn't know about any of the abuse I had suffered, was suffering, and so it was all just one big lie. I started to feel like a fraud, like I was pulling one over on her.

I was at my wit's end and didn't know what else to do. If therapy didn't work, if even professionals couldn't help me, what else was there? Nothing seemed to work, and I was running out of options. I just kept feeling worse and worse.

My depression became so intense that I started having thoughts of suicide again. I made the mistake of mentioning this to my therapist. Mental health professionals take this seriously, of course, as they are required to report patients who pose a credible risk to themselves. My therapist had the office call Richard and get him down to the practice immediately.

He showed up looking at me as if to say, *What have you done? What did you say?*

They told him about my suicidal ideation and said I needed to go to the hospital for further evaluation. Richard actually looked relieved that this wasn't about something I had disclosed about him, so initially he showed some sympathy.

He tried to console me while driving to the hospital. It didn't help, and I was still crying as he checked me in. They let him accompany me into the room, which is when it dawned on him where we were. This wasn't just a hospital. There was another patient wandering around in a gown, looking zonked out on meds. We were in the psychiatric ward where they kept inpatients.

Richard flipped out. He found the staff.

"She's not staying here," he said. "She is not crazy. She doesn't belong with these people."

But it was too late. I had already been admitted, and they were not going to let me leave since I was a danger to myself.

Richard glared at me, his face saying, *Look what you did now.*

TEN

THE COMMITTED WIFE

spent three weeks in the psych ward. They put me on meds that dulled my senses and calmed me down but left me feeling flat and hollow.

My stay there was boring and isolating. Richard refused to come see me at all. My mother didn't come to visit either, though my dad did show up one day during visitation.

"Julie, I understand why you'd want to kill yourself, I do," he said. There was a subtle implication that he wished I didn't feel this way, though he didn't say that explicitly.

His words struck me as odd. Why would he think he understood anything about my feelings? There was no reason for him to say something like this unless he was tacitly acknowledging the abuse I suffered at his hand. He was likely telling me, in code, that he understood where things had started to go wrong for me, but since we never spoke about this—not then, not ever—it's impossible for me to say so with certainty.

My stint in the psych ward was no more useful than therapy had been. They gave us daily evaluations and therapy sessions, in which the staff pushed me to open up about what was wrong. They asked the same sort of questions my therapist had asked: Where was this all coming from? Why was I self-harming? Why did I want to die?

My life was still my life, and, at some point, I was going to have to go home and face Richard again. I couldn't talk about the problems in my marriage with them any more than I could with my therapist, so I made up answers to their questions and pretended not to know what was making me so unhappy.

They clearly were not buying any of it, but with me unwilling to talk, they were at a loss, unable to help me. So, after three weeks, they sent me home with several prescriptions since there was nothing more they could do for me.

BACK INTO THE FRYER

The medications did not lead to any long-lasting relief because they were effectively a Band-Aid, numbing me without actually addressing the root of my problems, which was my life. Returning to the same dire reality, I had the same response. I made it maybe a month out of the hospital before becoming suicidal again.

This time around, I was determined to actually follow through with killing myself, and I now had the means for doing so. My prescriptions included several powerful sedatives. I was going to drive up into the mountains and find a secluded spot to down all of my pills at once with a whole bottle of liquor. No more messing around with an air conditioner now that I had both the means and the determination to go through with it.

Nothing sounded more pleasant than alcohol and pills carrying me off into an eternal sleep, forever. I dreamed about it all day long, taking great comfort in the knowledge that there was a way out, one that I could hold in my hand and rattle in the bottle.

I was still going to therapy as part of my ongoing treatment. In a moment of weakness, I made the mistake of telling my therapist about these daydreams, and bam, the same thing happened again. They called Richard to come back down. They wanted to send me back to the hospital again.

This time, Richard was not sympathetic at all. He stormed into the therapist's office, absolutely furious with me.

"Why are you doing this again?" he ranted. "This is so humiliating."

Richard drove me to the hospital, yet again, as they might have taken me by ambulance and billed us at the house otherwise. This time, he sat stewing in the car and wouldn't come in with me. I opened the door and went in on my own as he drove away.

I spent two more weeks in another hospital before they again sent me home with more meds. Richard seemed to have lost all respect for me after this second stint in the psych ward. He had never shown me much respect regardless, but now it was as though he didn't even see me as fully human. I was just an embarrassment to him, to the whole family, fundamentally broken.

Richard didn't trust me with my own meds, the various benzodiazepines and antidepressants prescribed to help me with my mood and difficulty sleeping. He confiscated them from me and dispensed them himself, forcing me to open my mouth to show that I had swallowed them, just as the nurses had done in the psychiatric ward.

Richard exercised this power over me in truly atrocious ways. Sometimes he gave me more of the meds than was prescribed and I blacked out, only to wake to him having sex with me. At the time, I didn't have the self-esteem to call this what it was—rape—but I felt violated.

Our "relationship" was nonexistent by this point, defined almost entirely by his abuse of me. We had few interactions that didn't involve his demeaning or humiliating me, often sexually. Our marriage was a joke, a sham.

I suspected him of having an affair, as he often stayed out late after work, giving reasons that sounded hollow. It was clear that he was lying, but I didn't press him on the point. There was way too much going on in my life to deal with more problems, so I looked the other way. I didn't love Richard anymore, if I ever actually had, so what did it matter? The more time he spent with someone else, hopefully the less time he had to force himself on me.

My parents were also disgusted with me for going back to the hospital again. The kids had been staying with them while

I was in the hospital, since my mom knew how little atten-tion Richard paid them. She was worried about him neglect-ing them, and since she probably suspected he was abusing me, not having me around to protect the children might have put them at greater risk as well. This also meant that she had to raise my children in place of me for several weeks, which had her feeling put out.

I would later find out that Richard was telling them lies about me while I was in the hospital. He characterized me as danger-ous and unstable, actually claiming that he was scared of *me* hurting the kids. These lies convinced my parents to side with him even more than usual, as they were concerned about what he had reported about me, none of which was true. I wasn't a danger to anyone but myself at that point, and certainly not a danger to my children.

Regardless, my parents had a poor opinion of me to begin with. Richard told me my mom thought my mental health crises were just my way of getting a break from the kids. It hurt my feelings that she thought I would ever stoop so low, but it was also just ridiculous. Psych wards are not Fiji; my time there was frightening and dehumanizing.

Richard also weaponized the whole experience against me, warning that he now had everything he needed to win the kids in a custody battle if I ever tried to leave him. He threatened to take them away and never let me see them again, which seemed like a credible threat since he was the kind of person to follow through—at least when it came to cruelty and vindictiveness.

I knew that he was right; he really did have all the ammo he needed. I couldn't keep myself out of the mental hospital—what judge was going to trust me with my children?

While this made me feel ever more trapped in the marriage, it also served as a strong motivator to pull myself together. I had to be healthy and good and happy, not just for myself, but also for my kids. I didn't want to lose them, nor could I kill myself and leave them alone with Richard. I had to stay strong for them.

The threat of losing my children helped me keep it together through the rest of the year, but it eventually became too much again. By the following summer, in 2007, I was suicidal yet again. Kaylee was now almost two years old, and the other two were just two years apart, so they were all very young still. Just looking at them made me cry—made me feel like the failure that Richard told me I had become. I wanted to be well, for them, but I just *wasn't* well.

HOME THERAPY

My therapist and the doctors at the hospital had alerted a family crisis service about my situation upon releasing me from the hospital a second time, and I was assigned a therapist who came to the house to work with me in my own environment. This was their last-ditch effort to fix me. The home service therapists were part of the hospital's critical care team who are only sent out when nothing else works and they have no idea what else to do with you.

This didn't mean that they were particularly helpful to me, though, as it was still impossible to talk about my real problems without breaking Richard's sacrosanct rules of secrecy. He was usually out of the house during my session, either at work or with whomever he was seeing on the side, but he would be home eventually, wanting to know what we had talked about.

So when the therapist asked about my problems, I continued to deflect. I insisted that I was fine, no matter the internal turmoil I felt.

When nothing worked to get me talking, and it never did, he would instruct me to watch movies, write down the plotlines, and talk about them in session. He was trying to help me find some glimmer of joy in life, something to live for, even if it was just simple escapist pleasures. But I couldn't find joy, couldn't find hope, and my mental health continued to deteriorate. I felt worn out and didn't know how much longer I could hold on for the kids' sake.

This was becoming more and more obvious with time, as I found it more and more difficult to keep up appearances. This was even apparent to Richard, who was home one night on a particularly bad night when I couldn't do much of anything other than rock on the sofa and cry to myself. When he couldn't even elicit a response from me, he called the therapist to come over and try to talk to me.

The therapist tried to coax me into talking, but what was there to say? Nothing I was actually allowed to voice, and I was too distraught at that point to even form sentences. The therapist tried to get me on the exercise bike, just to calm me down, but I couldn't even pedal. My whole body was heavy, as if I were underwater with weights strapped to my feet. I could barely even hold myself upright.

At this point, the therapist said that it was time to get me back to the hospital. "She's not doing well."

"Well, I'm not taking her," Richard said. "If she's going to the hospital, you're going to have to."

The therapist was taken aback. "What?"

"Yeah, I'm not doing this again," Richard said. "This is just ridiculous. It's pathetic. I'm not going to waste my time with this again."

Stunned, the therapist replied, "Okay, I guess I'll take her. I don't know if that's in my job description, or even allowed, but I'll try."

Richard got back on the computer and didn't say anything while the therapist walked me out the door. He got me into the car and helped buckle me in.

"I cannot believe your husband is making me drive you to the hospital," he said.

I was crying too hard to even respond or thank him, but it was still mortifying, even in my state, to have my husband refuse to care for me in a crisis.

(LOCKED) DOWN AND OUT

The therapist took me to a different hospital this time, a facility that specifically dealt with mental and behavioral health problems and was not part of a larger medical center. Addicts and alcoholics were in one wing, and everyone else, including me, was in the other wing. This hospital had more of an institutional feel, so much so that it was almost like a prison.

Upon admittance, I was subjected to a cavity search and seizure of my phone and other property. They issued me pants and a gown to wear and took me to a private holding room with nothing other than a bed that didn't even have bedsheets, as these could be tied into a noose. Everything was bolted down, including the bed and counters. There was a camera up in the corner of the room, watching me at all times.

The psychiatrist on duty was a tyrant, a short little man with anger problems. He was no help at all, actively making things worse. He took offense at my voice, which had always been naturally high-pitched and became squeaky in times of stress. He accused me of talking in a "baby voice" and refused to see me again until I was ready to "talk like a grown woman."

In such a bad headspace, I just said okay and slunk out of his office in tears.

A nurse passing by asked me what was wrong, and I told her it didn't matter. "I'm just going to kill myself."

This was a mistake, as they weren't going to let that slide. I was put on suicide watch, which meant staff had to be present at all times. There was someone standing by while I was using the toilet or shower. They even had me under observation while sleeping.

I was utterly isolated. Contact with the outside world was limited to ten minutes on a landline per day. Visitations could be arranged, but I had no one to visit. At this point, my entire family was furious with me and had no interest in visiting me, not even my dad. Whatever responsibility he may have felt for the trauma he had inflicted on me must have dissipated.

My mom was so disgusted with me for being back in the hospital that she wouldn't even readily take phone calls. She would no longer even do me the courtesy of talking behind my back. She told me exactly what she thought, which was that this whole situation was just my way of getting a little vacation from my kids.

Richard wouldn't really talk on the phone either. He sounded disinterested and distant on the other end of the line—not just distracted, but like he didn't even care.

He asked how I was doing, trying to gauge when they might let me out.

"I'm not doing well," I said.

There was a long pause. We exchanged a few banal statements until Richard eventually said he had to go.

The institution was utterly depressing and wholly ineffective. It was the kind of place that made you want to kill yourself, not live. The whole mental health system, I was learning, was not actually conducive to mental health, but I was trapped in it now.

The psychiatrist I had seen wanted to have me committed, which is a life-altering legal action stripping people of many of their rights. Having been committed follows you around for the rest of your life, as you have to report every day to take your pills at a dispensary. It's almost as bad as having a felony record, or worse in some ways since the state no longer treats you as a competent and free adult. There was another woman in the hospital who had lost her kids after being committed; they deemed her a hazard to them.

I couldn't let that happen to me, so I wrote a letter to the psychiatrist telling him everything he wanted to hear. There was an ambulance coming within the hour to take me in for processing to start the commitment process, so I had nothing to lose.

Lord, how I lied. I wrote everything that man wanted to hear. I wrote that he had totally cured me, that I was no longer depressed, that I didn't want to die, and that everything was better now. It had all been a temporary crisis, just a really bad couple of days, and, by the way, he was completely right: I was acting like a child. I was better now, all better, a competent and functional adult who needed to get back to her kids. I wanted him to believe that he had—single-handedly—cured me of all my problems.

I gave him the letter and hoped for the best. They called me in a little while later, I assumed to have me committed, but the psychiatrist had my letter in hand.

"Do you really mean all of this?" he asked.

"Yeah, of course I do," I said. "I'm better now."

It worked. I had stroked that man's ego. Not only was the ambulance called off, but they also released me that same day.

ELEVEN

THE TREATMENT OF LAST RESORT

Though the conditions at this last psychiatric ward were dehumanizing, I wasn't exactly thrilled to be going back home either. Richard was furious when he picked me up from the hospital. He sat me down at the house to let me know how it was going to be moving forward.

"This was the last time," he said, his anger palpable. "You're not going back to the hospital on my dime. No more of this."

Those were the new rules: no more hospitals, no more therapists. This was fine by me, as therapists hadn't helped, and institutions were unbearable. The truth, I had come to realize, was that nothing could change how I felt inside because the problem was external to me. The problem wasn't me; it was my actual life circumstances, my husband, his casual cruelty and micro-management of my existence.

Since there was no changing those circumstances, the only thing to do was suck it up. If I couldn't be happy, then I had to *pretend* to be happy. Fake it since you'll never make it. Depression wasn't allowed, so I was no longer depressed, period. By sheer force of will, I would be a happy wife and perfect mother, not crazy, not depressed.

This worked, for a while. I was more functional and took better care of the kids. I stopped crying, at least around them and Richard, since crying was no longer allowed. I kept it behind closed doors, in the bathroom, in the closet, anywhere out of sight. Dinner was waiting for Richard when he got home, and I kept the kids quiet while he was on the computer or in front of the television.

None of this made his treatment of me any kinder or less abusive, but, for a while, I was able to keep the peace and that was life.

Predictably, this was not sustainable. If this was my life now, then life wasn't worth living. Suicide became the rational choice. I had exhausted all of my other options. Hospitals were out, therapists were forbidden, I wasn't allowed to seek help, and I couldn't live this way—what else could I do?

Killing myself still meant forsaking my kids, but I told myself they were young and would hardly remember me when they got older. I rationalized it by pretending they'd be better off without me. My mom could take custody, as Richard wouldn't even want them once they no longer served the function of pawns to be used against me.

These thoughts made it easier to stomach having to leave them behind, but the truth was just that I couldn't keep doing this, not even for them. I didn't have it in me anymore. I wanted to, but I just couldn't.

"ESCAPE ONE LAST TIME"

Richard and I often took four-wheelers down into the canyon on day trips. We had been out on a ride recently when I spotted a man out on a cliff. He had climbed down onto a rock and was standing up on his tiptoes like a diver, as if he were about to jump. It must have been a thousand feet down to the bottom.

I pointed him out to Richard.

"He's going to kill himself," Richard said.

We stopped on the side of the road and crawled out over the rocks on our bellies because it was so dangerous to try to get within earshot of the man. When we could see him down below, we called out to ask whether he needed help. We tried to talk him off the rock, but the man just stared straight ahead, as if he couldn't even hear us, so Richard dialed 911.

Police and first responders showed up and shut down the whole canyon. There were cruisers and ambulances everywhere, along with a fire truck. They spent hours trying to talk him off the ledge, so long that I left to take the kids home. Richard came home later and told me the police ended the standoff by tackling the man and taking him in, probably to one of the same psychiatric hospitals where I had stayed.

Since I was suicidal, Richard kept bringing up this story. "Don't be like that guy, wasting everyone's time and all those resources for nothing. If you're going to do it, just do it."

This was cruel, but he had a point. I kept thinking, *Don't screw this up, not again. Do it right this time.* I spent the next month devising concrete plans to end my life, plans that would see me through to the end.

Devising an actual plan rendered my death less of an abstraction, which was sad for me to think about. I was sitting out on the back patio one day, watching the kids play while contemplating what to make them for breakfast on our last morning together. The thought caused me to break down and start crying, but thankfully Richard wasn't around to see.

When the morning of the big day finally arrived, I tried my best to act normal so as to not tip him off. I had made a doctor's appointment, which I did not intend to be alive for, and had plans to drop the kids off with Richard's grandparents. After sending Richard off to work, I got them dressed and took them to his grandmother's house, lying about being back in a few hours. I hugged and kissed them goodbye one last time and left. Though in tears the whole way home, I was determined to see this through.

Back at the house, I ran a bath before heading out. In the idealized vision of my own death, my body was clean and nicely dressed when it was found. So I soaked for a good long while before doing my hair, slipping on a nice dress, and picking out strappy dress sandals to match. I looked myself over in the mirror and, pleased, tossed my journal into a garbage bag along with some box cutters and an MP3 player before leaving the house.

I drove to the mountains outside of town, down near the same canyon where we had seen the man on the cliff, parked, and started hiking up the mountain. Though a popular trail, this was during the workday, so there weren't many people out. This was a good thing because the few hikers who were out on the trail shot me funny looks. I must have looked strange hiking in a cocktail dress and dress sandals, a garbage bag slung over my shoulder. Nobody stopped me, though; they just passed on by.

This was something of a disappointment, if I was being honest with myself, and I started to have doubts. *Am I making a mistake? Is this actually best for the kids or just easiest for me?* Suicide is a mistake you cannot ever undo: the mistake to end all mistakes, quite literally.

The number for a suicide prevention hotline was saved on my phone. I decided to call the number while trudging up the trail. This was my way of surrendering to fate, or God. If I wasn't meant to kill myself, then some divine presence would surely intervene through the voice of whoever picked up the line.

The phone rang a few times before the call was picked up. The man on the other end was nice, though he hardly sounded like any angel. He asked why I had called. I wouldn't say. I gave only brief answers, a word or two, no more, as I was too distraught to hold a conversation. I told him I was going to kill myself but wouldn't say why and wouldn't divulge my location. He couldn't get anything out of me.

His patience eventually wore thin. "Well, listen, if you're not going to tell me who you are or where to find you, I guess there's nothing we can do for you."

The phone clicked. He had hung up on me. I took this as a literal sign from God and the universe that suicide was the correct choice, the only choice.

I couldn't do it out in the open where someone might happen by and try to stop me, so I went off-trail and crossed a small creek before coming to a meadow in the woods. *As good a place as any*, I thought. It was certainly better than some psychiatric hospital; it was a peaceful place to die.

I sat down in the grass, took out my journal, and started drafting a goodbye letter, addressed to my kids, apologizing for abandoning them. I wanted them to know this had nothing to do with them, only me and my own failures. I didn't mention Richard for fear he would keep the letter from them.

When I was done, I put on my headphones, laid back in the grass, and put Sarah McLachlan's "Angel" on, which seemed appropriate as a send-off. I listened to the whole song, start to finish, and then took out the box cutters and carved my children's initials into my thigh—R.A.K. I cut so deep my thigh still bears the scar to this day. The pain didn't matter, only that I left the mark, indelible. I wanted whoever found me, the coroner, everyone, to know my last thoughts were of my children.

After carving their initials into my thigh, I hiked even farther into the woods to find a secluded area where no one could find me until the deed was done. The last thing I needed was someone trying to stop me—or worse, revive me. My method of suicide was asphyxiation, and I wanted to die, not come out brain damaged.

I had prepared a plastic grocery bag by covering it in thick packing tape so that it couldn't be torn by hand. I checked the bag with my hands, testing the tape against my fingers and thumb, before tying it in place over my head. I laid back in the grass and waited to drift off calmly into nothingness.

Only it wasn't the peaceful send-off I had envisioned. As oxygen ran out, panic set in and the fight-or-flight response took over. My hands tore at the bag frantically, but the bag wouldn't come off. I had quadruple knotted it around my neck and the tie wouldn't give, but I was able to force my fingers past the tape and through the bag to let air in.

Suddenly, I could breathe again—and I *hated* it, hated myself for it. I was crying now, hysterical at my failure. *You can't even kill yourself right.* I felt like the most ridiculous, pathetic person to have ever lived.

I ripped the bag off from around my neck and hopelessly tossed it aside. It was worthless now. I still had the box cutters, but slitting my wrists was too hard, too scary. I had tried in the past, but the blood was too much for me and it was impossible for me to cut deep enough to hit the artery.

Utterly defeated, I headed back down the trail, sobbing hysterically, blood running down my thigh. Branches and brambles tore at my legs and tattered my dress as I shambled through the woods, but I didn't care. It was as if I were on cruise control, my mind unable to keep pace with what my body was doing. I had no plan, couldn't even conceive of one, couldn't even conceive of the act of planning itself.

When I reached the trail, I crossed paths with a hiker, unlikely in the afternoon on a workday, so maybe here was the guardian angel I had been looking for...but I was no longer interested, didn't want to be saved, had no use for serendipity at this point.

"Are you okay?" he asked, his eyes glancing at the blood streaming down my leg.

I was crying too hard to answer. He led me over to a rock and sat me down.

"Can I use your cell phone?" I stammered, the only thing I was capable of getting out.

My hands were trembling too much to actually take the phone from him, and I wouldn't have been able to talk on it anyway.

"Should I call someone?" he asked.

I gave him Richard's number and listened while he tried to explain the situation. Just imagining Richard's face on the other end was enough to snap me back to reality.

The man hung up the phone. "He's on his way. I can wait with you until he gets here."

Richard was going to be so furious that I would *wish* I had killed myself, so furious he would want to finish the job for me. Unable to bear the thought of seeing him, of facing up to all of that, I took off running down the trail.

The man darted after me, easily catching up in a few bounds, and tackled me to the ground. He apologized but said that he couldn't in good conscience let me go off on my own like this. I struggled against him.

"Please, you're not going to get away," he said. "I played football."

I begged him to let me go. He didn't understand, and, as per usual, I couldn't explain why, so I just begged and begged, but he held me there, insisting it was for my own good.

What felt like forever passed while we waited on Richard, this stranger holding my hand the whole time, trying to calm me down. If he had any success there, it was undone the moment Richard came walking up the hill, dragging the boys behind him, with Kaylee up on his shoulders. Knowing I had just tried to kill myself, Richard had taken it upon himself to stop and pick up the kids so he could march them two miles up a trail to see me like this.

"You brought the kids?" I cried in disbelief.

I tried to bolt again, but the man grabbed my arm and wouldn't let go, though he seemed startled by the kids as well. He had made the situation clear to Richard on the phone. I was caked in blood.

"She's going to run," he shouted to Richard. "Take the kids down. They really shouldn't see this."

Richard stared at him defiantly, like who does this guy think he is? "No, we're here to pick her up."

"Well, then I'll take them down," the guy offered, looking to me to see if that was okay.

I nodded yes, please, and he walked the kids down the mountain, back to the parking lot at the base of the trail. Richard didn't try to stop him, perhaps happy to be rid of this intruder. Once he disappeared down the trail, Richard marched over, madder than hell, and, without saying much of anything, grabbed ahold of my ear. He walked me down the mountain, pinching my ear the whole way, like I was a misbehaving child or escaped livestock. He didn't yell, didn't speak; he was too mad to say anything at all.

When we got back to the parking lot, the man waiting with my kids looked distraught. Richard had quickly let go of my ear when we emerged from the trees, but the man had already seen.

While Richard was loading the kids into the car, the man came and slipped me his cell phone number on a piece of paper. "If you ever need help, please just let me know."

Having finished with the kids, Richard was waiting in the car, just glaring at me. He must have overheard us because as soon as I was in the car, he demanded the piece of paper I had been given. He ripped it to shreds right in front of me.

"You're such an attention whore," he sneered. "All you ever want is people to pay attention to you."

UNPROFESSIONAL HELP

Richard drove straight back to his grandmother's house to drop off the kids, which made it even clearer that there was no reason to have collected them in the first place except to humiliate me at their expense. My two boys were old enough to be traumatized by this ordeal, but Richard didn't care. He just wanted to hurt me, no matter the collateral damage.

After dropping off the kids, he drove me back to the hospital even though he had previously said no more hospitals. This was the first hospital we had come to, so I knew it well. He dragged me into the emergency room to be seen but couldn't wait for an evaluation to start screaming in my face.

"What is wrong with you? Why can't you be normal?" he demanded. "What is so wrong with your life? Nothing. You're just a failure! I'm sick of it. I can't do this anymore."

He went on and on. My inability to respond with anything but tears only made him angrier.

"Look at what you did!" he said, swatting the open wound on my thigh.

This drove the hospital staff, passively watching the situation escalate, to finally intervene. They told him to back off now that he had hurt me and assigned a security guard to watch over my room, which was a relief. The counselors finally did my evaluation, determining that I had to be admitted since I posed an active risk of harm to myself. Richard said, "Good," and left me there crying in the emergency room.

Although this wasn't the worst hospital I had seen the inside of, it was still no walk in the park. During intake, I was interviewed by another counselor who ended up being a total creep. He asked all the usual questions—"What's wrong?" "How do you feel?" "Why are you depressed?"—before getting weird. He hesitated, shifted in his seat, and then gave me a serious look.

"I need you to be honest about something," he said. "Do you masturbate? Is that what this is about?"

"No," I said, disgusted by how inappropriate he was being.

"You can tell me," he said. "How often do you masturbate?"

He wouldn't let up, repeatedly pressing me for details about the "truth," but I told him no, no, no and that he needed to stop. He threatened not to admit me into the hospital, which was frightening given the prospect of going back to the house with Richard so upset. Thankfully it was a hollow threat, and I was ultimately admitted.

They put me straight into lockdown, in a room where I couldn't even go to the bathroom without staff standing guard. The room was basically empty, save for the bed, which I didn't even use. I just lay down on the tile floor because, in my mind, a bed was more than someone like me deserved. I couldn't even kill myself right. I deserved the hard floor where I could die like a dog. For days, I did little more than lie there and cry, refusing to move on my own for anything, not even for meals. They set out a tray of food beside me on the floor at mealtime so I could roll over and take a few bites. Mostly, I had no appetite and ate little.

Richard refused to speak with me throughout my entire stay, my parents likewise. I was more alone than ever this time.

Conveying the depth of my hopelessness to anyone who hasn't felt the same is hard. Words simply fail. My heart hurt so much I would have torn it out of my chest if I had had the means. I didn't want to be in this place. I didn't want to be *anywhere*—not in a hospital, not at home, not on this earth. I wanted to be dead and gone, and I had no faith in their ability to help me, not anymore. No one could help me, that much was clear, which was why I was no longer speaking to any staff.

The only nurse I would confide in was a middle-aged woman who saw me crying alone. The therapists must have told her that I wasn't talking because she came up to say she was quitting her job and that this was her last shift.

"You'll never see me again," she said. "If you want to tell me what's really going on, I'll listen and promise to take it with me to the grave. I won't tell anyone."

Her gentle demeanor helped me let my guard down, and, for the first time in my life, I opened up to someone about what was going on. I told her my husband was abusing me, something I had never told anyone. Weeping, I told her he was threatening to take my kids away, so I was trapped in the marriage.

She listened and tried to comfort me. Just opening up to someone, finally, was cathartic and made me feel a little less alone. Though I begged her to swear not to tell anyone, for fear of it getting back to Richard, part of me hoped she would do so because it would have forced me to confront the issue. However, she was a woman of her word and never told anyone. No one at the hospital said anything to indicate they were aware of my disclosure, and I never saw her again.

After a week or so, the hospital sent me home with more prescriptions, the same as last time. I was told there was nothing else they could do for me, which I already knew.

TWELVE

LIVE TO WORK? NO, WORK TO LIVE

ack at the house, fresh from my latest stay at the psychiatric hospital, I was forced to listen as Richard sat me down yet again, this time not just telling me how things were going to be from now on but also giving me a firm ultimatum.

"Enough is enough," he said. "You either get better, and things go back to the way they used to be, or we are done."

He didn't actually mean to *get* better. He meant to *be* better—he wanted me cured, now. No more hospitals, no more therapy, no more medications, no more treatments of any kind. I just had to be cured. If I wasn't, it was game over for our marriage and he was taking the kids with him. He reminded me that all my stays in the hospital would make it clear to the state how unfit I was to have custody of the kids.

What choice did I have? "Be better" or lose my kids? I told him, "Okay, I'm better now."

Stopping my medications cold turkey sent me immediately into hellish withdrawals—fatigue, strange headaches, tremors, and more—but I struggled through without complaint since that would not be tolerated. I once again willed myself to be happy, to stop crying, to act as if everything was okay.

But, of course, everything was not okay. Though demanding perfect mental health of me, Richard continued treating me abusively. In fact, consistent with his treatment of me after my previous hospital stays, the abuse only became worse.

Though he didn't want me going to the hospital again, it was clear that Richard thought I was fundamentally sick and broken. He turned the house into my own private insane asylum. He put a lock on the bathroom door in our bedroom and wore the key on a chain around his neck. This way he could put me on lock-down in the bathroom.

On several occasions, unprecipitated by anything on my end, he went into the bathroom, tore down the shower curtain, and ripped everything out of the cabinets before locking me in there by myself.

"Now try and hurt yourself," he would snarl.

The first time this happened, I tried to escape through the window, but it wouldn't open all the way. I was small, but not small enough to wiggle through.

Another time, he locked me in the bathroom and brought the kids into the bedroom to spank them. I could hear them crying and yelling for mommy, but I couldn't get to them, which was torture. That was the whole point—the punishment was mine more than theirs.

"It'll be okay," I said, cheek pressed up against the door, trying to comfort them from the other side, but Richard told me to shut up unless I wanted them to get it worse.

Despite these clear instances of abusive behavior, Richard accused *me* of being a danger to the kids. He gathered up all the knives in the house and locked them in the gun safe because he was supposedly worried I would hurt the kids.

"You're going to kill the kids," he was always saying. "You're going to kill the kids, aren't you?"

This made no sense—being suicidal doesn't make you homicidal, and *he* was the one hurting the kids—but I was so susceptible to his mind games that I started to worry about their safety in my presence. *What if he's right? What if I am a danger to them?* It felt like my mind was starting to go.

Richard used "protecting the kids" from me as a pretext to start tying my leg to his at night so that I couldn't get up without him knowing. I was forced to sleep on my back so there would be enough slack in the rope in case he rolled over in the middle of the night. In the morning, I had to wait for him to wake before I could go to the bathroom. My sleep deteriorated—I couldn't sleep while literally shackled to him.

Richard eventually decided I was no longer worthy of sharing a bed with him and started forcing me to sleep on the floor by the nightstand, with no pillow and no blanket. He would occasionally reach down in the middle of the night to make sure I hadn't undone the knot in the rope and gotten away.

Living this way was intolerable. I no longer felt caged—I *was* caged, locked in the restroom, tethered to my abusive spouse. I couldn't even escape him when he was away at work. He claimed to have hidden cameras around the house so that he could keep an eye on me when he was out.

Feeling particularly spunky one day, I tested the claim by putting up my middle finger and waving it all around the room.

As if on cue, the phone started ringing. It was Richard.

"What did you just do?" he asked, coolly. In a tone a parent would use to address a misbehaving child, he added, "This will be easier on you if you just tell me."

I denied having done anything. For his part, Richard wouldn't come out and say what I had done. He wanted me to know that he knew, while also maintaining the pretense that there were no cameras.

THE PRESCHOOL

It became clear to me that staying in the house all day was not an option, not if I wanted to maintain my sanity. I got it in my mind to look for a job, even though this wasn't allowed under the terms of my contract with Richard. However, if he was going to let me out of the house for anything, it would be to bring home a paycheck. I just needed to find something where I could take my kids along since Richard was never going to pay for daycare.

Luckily, there was an opening for a teacher position at a nearby preschool. I submitted an application and went in for an interview. They hired me on the spot to join the faculty for the beginning of the 2007 school year, which was right around the corner. They even let me enroll my kids in preschool free of charge, so they could come with me to work.

It felt like my prayers had been answered. I loved children and had always wanted to teach preschool, so this was perfect. It would get both me and the kids out of the house. For their part, the kids didn't mind being there since it was better than being at home with their dad. For his part, Richard didn't mind me working, as he was glad to have me and the kids out of the house.

Things seemed like they might actually work out. I had found a way to be content with my life. For the first time since becoming a mother, or more accurately, since starting my relationship with Richard, I actually had something of a social life since there were other teachers and my boss to talk with at school. I loved the children in my class, and their parents were often highly engaged. This was the most interpersonal interaction I had had in years, ever really, and it was refreshing, which helped me shuck off the worst of my depression.

Life at home was still a struggle, of course, but I now had somewhere else to put my energy and attention. I stayed late every day, sometimes until midnight, just decorating or preparing lessons for the next day. I spent as much time at the school as possible to avoid being back at the house.

My favorite student was a girl named Bella who reminded me of myself, which wasn't necessarily a good thing. She was introverted, withdrawn even, so much so that she avoided eye contact. She didn't look up when spoken to, wouldn't talk to the other kids, and didn't participate in activities. She just sat there by herself, quietly. A sad little creature who looked miserable all the time. What worried me about Bella was that these were the same behaviors and mannerisms I had displayed growing up while being abused by my father. I worried the same thing was happening to her.

I voiced this concern to my boss, Teresa. She took the matter seriously but said we couldn't act without evidence. Making a false accusation against a parent, or anyone for that matter, would be terrible for everyone involved. A gut feeling wasn't proof.

For the time being, I simply took Bella under my wing, lavishing her with attention. I would hold her during class and eat meals with her sometimes. We grew closer, and she eventually started to come out of her shell a little, at least around me.

Naturally, we work closely with preschool parents, who drop the kids off and pick them up at the end of the day. Bella was usually driven to and from school by her parents, often her dad.

His name was Eric.

STALKED

At first, Eric was just another parent. Nothing stood out about him, aside from my worry over his daughter. Doting over Bella did mean that I spent more time with him than other parents, though, as I was concerned about her.

I didn't confront Eric about my suspicions directly, for obvious reasons, but instead simply voiced concern over how withdrawn Bella was in class. Eric was grateful to be alerted to the issue and to have someone showering his daughter with so much attention, and he later seemed relieved when she started to do better under my care. This was enough to mostly clear him as the perpetrator of any abuse, in my eyes, and while I still worried about Bella, Eric fell off my radar, especially since Bella was making progress.

When the holidays came around, the preschool threw a Christmas party for the kids and parents. We had made cardboard houses, and the kids were pretending to be Santa Claus. They tried to toss little beanbags into the chimneys from a distance. It was a lot of fun, but I was running around like a crazy person the whole time, pushing all the kids around in a plastic laundry basket serving as a makeshift sled.

Working up a sweat and out of breath, I hardly even noticed Eric there, but apparently *he* had taken note of *me*. He would later tell me that this was when he had "fallen" for me, which is to say he had developed an unhealthy obsession with me, as I was soon to find out.

In the spring, Bella suddenly stopped showing up for preschool. Worried, I called the home number we had on record, but no one answered. I was heartbroken. She had made so much progress, and I hated for her to miss the end of the school year.

It was several months later, near the end of the school year, when Eric finally showed up at school with Bella.

"Oh my gosh, is everything okay?" I asked. "Can I help in any way?"

Eric rubbed his neck, struggling to find the right words in English. "I'm having trouble getting her here, with work."

I wanted Bella back in school so badly, I offered to pick her up on the way to school in the mornings. The school year was almost over, and I already had to drive my three kids. What was one more? Eric gratefully obliged and gave me their address and his cell phone number. He asked me to text instead of calling, which I had never done. This was 2008, the first iPhone had just come out, and texting was still kind of new. Richard was always on his phone texting God knows who, as he was definitely having affairs by this point, but I had never had any use for texting since I had no friends to communicate with. So Eric took me aside and showed me how to send text messages.

I picked up Bella from his house four or five times over the course of the remaining school year. Eric would text me when she needed a ride, and I would text back okay. He had Bella ready to go, standing by the door with her backpack on.

If she wasn't ready yet, Eric would invite me inside, which caused the hair on the back of my neck to stand on end. Eric was married, or so he claimed, but his wife was never around in the morning, though I had met her previously at the school. The voice inside my head told me *do not go inside,* so I would make up some excuse about being in a hurry to get to school.

Eric could be persistent, and, not wanting to upset him, I eventually went inside one morning while Bella finished getting her shoes on. This made me feel terribly uncomfortable, as Richard didn't know I was helping Eric get Bella to school. He would have read into the situation and accused me of cheating, so this needed to remain a secret.

Despite my nervousness about stepping over the threshold, nothing happened. When Bella finished getting her things together, I picked her up and we were off. It was still a relief to be out of the house, as Richard would have killed me if he had known that I stepped inside.

This all seemed innocent enough, but Eric now had my cell phone number. At first, he just texted when he wanted me to pick up Bella, but there was always some follow-up comment about something else, just to get me texting back. This quickly turned into Eric initiating conversations over text that had nothing to do with Bella, which seemed inappropriate. We were supposed to have a professional relationship, not a personal one, but, per usual, I didn't have it in me to tell a man to stop, for fear of being mean and upsetting him.

Every time my phone buzzed at home, I had a small heart attack for fear of Richard finding out. Of course, he eventually did. My phone was sitting out at the house one day when it lit up from a text message. Richard saw it and got to the phone before I could. It was just an old flip phone, no passcode required, and he opened it up and started reading my messages.

Richard flew off the handle. "Who is this fucking guy?"

"He's just the dad of one of the kids," I said. "It's not a big deal."

"Well, he's not talking about school. He's talking to you like a friend," Richard said accusatorially, as if this were the worst thing in the world, that I might have *a friend*—the horror.

Richard went berserk, shouting and tossing his arms around, just ranting and raving about me "having an affair." I started crying hysterically, my mental state regressing instantly, so quickly that I blacked out while he was screaming. The matter was left unresolved.

The next day, I told Eric to stop texting me outside of regular work hours. I should have told him to stop completely, but I still wanted to ensure that Bella could get to school. I also didn't want to offer an explanation, which I would have had to do if I cut him off completely. To my surprise, he respected the request and stopped texting at night.

Unfortunately, he also started coming around the school after hours, which meant he somehow knew I had been staying late at work. In retrospect, it was clear that he only could have known this if he were watching me.

It began with him showing up one evening and offering to pick up dinner for me and the kids in his truck. Not wanting to upset him or acknowledge how weird it was that he knew we were there, I just let him grab us dinner, which was kind of nice but also strange and inappropriate. Why would he be buying us dinner? It felt like he was paying me way too much attention. But, again, I was too timid to turn him away.

This was a mistake. Eric started showing up in his truck almost every night, well after dark, sometimes as late as midnight. Now feeling stalked, I would turn out all the lights and hide in the back of the school to do my work. Eric would come up to the front door and knock persistently since he knew I was inside. My car was out front, so I wasn't fooling anybody, but I refused to answer and just waited until I could hear his truck pulling away.

This got so bad that I had to tell Teresa what was going on. She already knew something was strange about Eric. He had been calling the office and asking for me during the school day. When she tried to take a message, since I was teaching, he would just hang up and try back later, but she knew who it was from his voice and the caller ID.

Teresa was vaguely aware of how hard things had been for me, though not in any specific way, which was why she allowed me to stay at the school late and was very protective of me. Wanting to nip this in the bud right away, she sat down with me one day to write Eric a long text informing him that his recent behavior was unprofessional and needed to stop.

Teresa also barred him from coming to the preschool again, which left me feeling conflicted. Bella had made such progress, and now she wasn't going to finish the school year. This was a shame, but Eric had me at my wit's end. He was causing me trouble with Richard that I couldn't afford, not right now. My mental health was still incredibly fragile, too fragile to be dealing with all of this. It had to stop, and if Bella was collateral damage, that couldn't be helped, not by me.

Eric didn't respond to the text. He simply cut off contact and stopped bringing Bella to school without complaint. I felt incredibly guilty but also knew I had dodged a bullet.

I couldn't have been more wrong.

THIRTEEN

THE END OF A MARRIAGE

ince the preschool had become my refuge from home, the end of the school year presented a significant problem. I knew that spending all my time back at the house with nothing to distract me from my terrible marriage would send me spiraling back into depression and right back to the hospital again.

This wasn't an option, so I asked Teresa if I could teach summer school on my own. She graciously agreed, allowing me to use the space and even the supplies. I developed a summer school curriculum and advertised the program by hanging flyers around town. Enough parents signed up that I was able to keep teaching straight through the whole summer, which was a lifesaver, as my mental health depended on having some space from Richard.

However, this distance ultimately drove the last nail in the coffin for our relationship, which had continued to deteriorate. At this point, we were basically two people living in the same house, two roommates who despised each other. Any pretense of decency evaporated, and Richard began doing cruel things for no reason at all. Where before he had often made excuses and justifications for his behavior, now he offered none at all. He would stick out his elbow when we passed by each other, deliberately hitting my face just to hurt me.

Worse than the physical abuse was how he treated me and the kids. We were just an expense, one he was no longer all that interested in maintaining, as became abundantly clear when his biological father came to visit in September, around my birthday. Though raised by his mother and stepfather, Richard had reached out to his biological father years before with my encouragement.

Back in 2000, his father had flown us out to Disneyland to meet him and his wife, and afterward we went back to their house in Idaho. It quickly became clear that he was related to Richard, as he treated his wife tyrannically, ordering for her in restaurants and talking over her as though she didn't exist.

Richard now wanted to buy a big-screen television so he could watch NASCAR with his father when he visited. This was infuriating, given how Richard was always pinching pennies and acting as if we were broke. I laid into him for it, which was very much out of character for me, but I was just so angry at the self-indulgence of this purchase.

Richard didn't care. He bought the television anyway. Later that night, when I told him we needed to get milk for Kaylee, he said he had already spent all our money on the TV.

"What am I supposed to do about Kaylee?"

"Go ask the neighbors for milk," he said dismissively.

I literally walked around the neighborhood, begging for milk to fill my daughter's sippy cup while he hooked up his new television.

TO CATCH AN ADULTERER

By then, it was becoming ever clearer to me that the marriage was nearing its end. I couldn't go on this way much longer. I was getting depressed again and wasn't allowed to see anyone for it. I could not continue to live this way, so I decided to take the kids and leave.

I made plans to disappear in the middle of the night. There was already a bag packed and ready to go when I went upstairs to wake the kids. Unfortunately, young as they were, they were uncooperative and whined about being woken up, wanting to know where we were going. I tried to shush them, but to no avail. When Richard woke and came to see what all the commotion was about, I told him the kids were having nightmares. He didn't notice anything out of the ordinary and went back to bed, but I dared not try to leave with the kids now.

After trying another night only to have my plans foiled again, it was clear this wasn't going to work. After more thought, I realized that running off with the kids was a bad idea. Inevitably, Richard would sic the police on me and then paint me as the crazy kidnapper.

Richard already had so much to use against me in divorce proceedings and a custody battle. If I was ever going to get away with the kids, I would need ammunition of my own. I needed to be able to prove he was committing adultery.

My suspicions were long-standing. He was clearly interested in other women, as he had been pressing me to have a three-way encounter with him and had tasked me with finding another woman. The only person I knew outside of work was a woman across the street named Allison, who ran a daycare out of her house. We were barely friends, but we had bonded over our love for working with small children. Richard wanted me to talk her into joining us in the bedroom. The upside of this was that I was allowed to spend time at her house, though I certainly never tried to convince her to come to bed with us. I used the time at her place to learn how to socialize again and simply lied to Richard about what was taking so long. I told him she was warming up to the idea but needed a little more time to become comfortable.

Richard was furious with my lack of progress initially, but he ultimately dropped it as he got deeper into an affair with a woman from his online school. I overheard him having a conversation with her on the computer in which his tone was clearly flirtatious. This confirmed preexisting suspicions now that he was suddenly "staying late" at work and "going into the office" on Saturdays again.

Though I didn't care for him at all by this point, the affair was still upsetting to me. It saddened me that he would disrespect and betray me in this way, especially when I was struggling with my mental health. I had tolerated his affairs up until this point because it was better to have him out with some woman than at home yelling at me and the kids, but that didn't mean it didn't make me feel bad about myself.

I had started digging through the trash for receipts to catch him in his lies. He told me he had gotten Subway for lunch one day, but I found a receipt in the trash proving he had purchased two meals at a Chinese restaurant that afternoon. I filed these receipts away and started making notes, collecting evidence, and building my case against him for our future divorce proceedings. I was naive enough to think a judge would frown on his having an affair.

My naivete also had me hoping that catching Richard in an affair would bring my parents around to supporting my side. They were still disgusted with me for having gone to the hospital all those times but proving that Richard was cheating on me might be enough to turn them against him, or so I hoped.

My dad was helpful to this end—he actually put me in contact with someone he knew from the military who was now a private investigator. Certain my marriage was coming to an end, I had started squirreling away personal money on the sly, which was difficult given how tight Richard had gotten with money and how strictly he policed my spending. Thankfully, I had managed to save enough to hire the private investigator, and I couldn't think of a better use for the money than buying leverage to use in the divorce process. I needed a card of my own to play.

It didn't take the PI long to get all the proof I could ever need. He trailed Richard to a nearby house when he was supposedly "working late" and got pictures of a woman letting him inside. He also got pictures of them making out in the parking lot outside Richard's work. The PI called to let me know what he had found, and we made plans to meet the next Monday so I could collect the photos and pay him the remainder of my balance.

While I actively loathed Richard at this point, the stress of the affair, further proof of my failing marriage, had been taking its toll on me. I had become suicidal again, even before hiring the PI and getting definitive proof.

I was having a hard time one night when Richard was out, presumably with his girlfriend, and it all just seemed like too much. Suffering a breakdown, I got it in my head again to try to kill myself. Richard kept a loaded gun in the bedroom. Sometimes he would leave it out on the nightstand, which I interpreted as his desire for me to kill myself with it. I could never touch a gun, though. I decided I would simply slit my wrists in the shower and be done with it.

For whatever reason, I decided to line the tub with a painter's tarp, presumably to make it easier for whoever found me to clean up. In fact, peeling up the tarp was harder than simply rinsing my blood down the drain, but I wasn't exactly thinking clearly at the time. After prepping the shower, I got under the water with the box cutters in my hand, ready to do the deed, but a voice in my head was saying, *No, you can't do this. You can't do this. You need to reach out to somebody.*

I decided to call Allison across the street. We weren't really all that close, but there wasn't anyone else I could reach out to who wasn't a coworker. I gave her a call and asked for help. She could tell it was serious and came running across the street to find me in the shower.

"You can't do this," she said, helping me out of the shower and back into my clothes. She cleaned up the bathroom so no one could tell anything was amiss and sat me down at the kitchen table with a drink.

"How long has it been this bad?" she asked.

I told her my life story, leaving out the worst parts about Richard. She sat there, listening sympathetically. When I was done, she called Richard on his cell phone to have him come home. I was too out of it to try to stop her.

When she dialed Richard, he answered the phone, "Hey, babe."

"Excuse me?"

"Amy?"

"No, this is *Allison*, from across the street," she said. "I don't know who Amy is, but your wife is here trying to kill herself and you need to get home right now."

Richard rushed back, surely knowing he had been caught in an affair. Allison didn't tell me what he had said until much later, thinking me too fragile to hear about an affair at that time. By the time she did, I had already found incriminating emails while snooping on his computer and hired the private investigator, which gave me all the confirmation and proof I could ever need.

THE BRUISE

The Monday I was supposed to pick up the photos from the private investigator, the thirteenth of October, I came home from work feeling too depressed to go out. It was all becoming too much for me again—the affairs, Eric stalking me over the spring, Richard's cruelty.

Richard found me lying on the couch, looking absolutely terrible, which was also how I felt inside.

"What the fuck is wrong with you?" he said.

"I'm just really sick."

"Well, you better not be sick in the head. This better be a *real* sickness."

I lied and told him it was. "I'm going to bed."

I went upstairs and got in bed and just lay there, feeling too sad to move for several hours. When the door creaked open and Richard came in, I pretended to be asleep. He lay down next to me and, out of nowhere, kicked me extremely hard in the shin with the back of his foot, clearly on purpose.

I yelped and jumped up. "What was that for?"

Richard was quiet for a long moment. When he finally spoke, his voice was surprisingly measured, as if he really meant what he had to say. "I just hate you so much," he said. "I just hate you."

The words hung in the air. He eventually rolled over and pulled the sheets over himself. I lay there staring at the back of his head, my heart pounding in my chest. He had never hit me so hard before.

He's going to kill me, I thought. *I have to get out of this.*

The next day, I had a doctor's appointment for something unrelated, a standard checkup. My leg had developed a giant bruise overnight where Richard had kicked me, having turned all black and blue and swollen. Though I could have worn pants, I picked out a skirt to put on before heading to the doctor, hoping someone would see the bruise. I would never be able to bring up the abuse on my own, so this was my weak attempt to force the issue.

My usual doctor was out of the office, so they had me see an intern. During the appointment, I crossed my legs, allowing the skirt to ride up over the bruise. The intern spotted it immediately.

"That's a nasty bruise," he said. "How'd you get that?"

When I started crying, he came and sat near me.

"You can tell me," he said softly. "It's okay."

Telling my family doctor would have been impossible, as he knew Richard, but this person was a stranger, which made me feel safe enough to admit my husband had kicked me. Maybe it was just desperation, but I was so sad, and so mad, and just needed to tell someone.

"You need to report this to the police," he said.

"What? No."

"Here's the thing," he said. "I have to report this. Either you go to the police, or I do."

I was stunned, in complete shock, and started crying harder upon realizing my mistake. "It's nothing. I'm fine. Just forget about it."

But he was adamant. Either I went to the police, or he would. He told me my husband didn't have to know. The police would just photograph the bruise and document the incident in a file. Naive as I was, I believed him. It would turn out to be one more piece of evidence to use against Richard in a future custody battle.

I went straight from the doctor's office to the police station and told the police my husband had kicked me.

"I just want to report it for my file," I said, trying to sound both casual and confident.

They had me wait on a wooden bench in the lobby until an officer could come take my statement. While waiting, I started to have second thoughts. My whole body began shaking with anxiety; I worried this was a terrible mistake. If Richard found out, he would kill me, literally kill me for this one. But the doctor had given me an ultimatum, so what choice did I really have?

An officer came and took me into a private room. He took notes while I gave my statement. They wanted to have the crime scene investigators take pictures, so I went back to the lobby to wait on the bench.

This was complete agony, and I was about to jump out of my skin when my phone buzzed. I opened it up to see a message asking if I was okay. The sender claimed to have a strange feeling something was wrong; he claimed to be inspired by God to reach out to me at that moment. I didn't recognize the number at first and sat staring at the texts, dumbfounded, racking my brain over who this could be until it dawned on me.

Eric.

It had been about eight months since I had heard from him. He hadn't texted me, hadn't come around the school, nothing. He had just disappeared...until now.

Why was he reaching out to me now, at this exact moment? That it was just a coincidence seemed a stretch, but I was too shaken up from giving the police my statement to dwell on the fact. I just replied no, everything was fine, but I couldn't talk now. He wrote back okay and said he would check in with me later.

Before I could contemplate this any further, the investigators came to photograph my bruise. I posed while they took clinical shots of my leg.

Afterward, the first officer sat me back down and told me they were acting on my report. Two officers were en route to Richard's work to arrest him for battery. I collapsed straight to the floor, sobbing, begging them not to do this.

"You don't understand. He's going to kill me. He can't know I was here. I just wanted to document it, that's all. Please don't arrest him!"

They told me it wasn't up to me anymore. They were pressing charges. It was between him and the city now.

Done with my statement and photos, I was free to go. I stumbled out into the daylight in a complete panic, not wanting to be at the station when they came back with Richard. My life was unraveling right before me, and even though it was happening so fast, everything seemed to move in slow motion.

Despite the shock, I was able to think surprisingly clearly. This time, my marriage was definitely over; that much was clear. The first thing Richard would do after posting bond would be to cut me off financially. Everything was in his name—all our money, all our accounts, everything. I would be immediately destitute.

I went to the bank and convinced a bank associate to add me to our checking account. There was only $4,000 in the account, so either Richard had blown all our money, or he was keeping it elsewhere. I wasn't sure which. Not wanting to leave him totally high and dry, I pulled out $3,000 in cash—one grand for each of the kids—and left a thousand for him.

From there, I went to get the kids from Richard's grandmother. She didn't seem to know anything was amiss, so I collected them without incident and went back to the house to wait.

And wait.

And wait.

And wait...

It was absolute agony not knowing what was happening with Richard. Was he being held overnight? Had he posted bond? Without knowing, I didn't feel safe in the house.

Not knowing where else to turn, I phoned my mom and filled her in about what was going on. She was livid, absolutely furious with me. She started screaming into the phone so loudly that her voice distorted into static.

"How could you do this to him?" she shouted. "After all you've put him through, with the hospitals and everything, and now this. I can't believe you!"

I just sat there crying, listening to her tell me how horrible she thought I was.

"I want to see you *now*," she demanded, "to figure this out."

The idea of seeing her in person was too much, too terrible. I wouldn't do it, not at the house, not without a neutral arbiter. The only place I was willing to meet her was in therapy. She resisted at first, demanding to come to the house, but I wasn't going to let her in, so she finally agreed to meet at my therapist's office. I had scheduled an emergency session, explaining the situation to my therapist, and headed over there with the kids. They sat in the lobby, playing with toys and stuffed animals while I met with my mom in the back.

I had never seen my mom so mad, not in my whole life, not in my presence. She went red in the face bellowing about how awful I was being to Richard, a good man by her account. She made the case against me to my therapist, who was sticking up for me as my mom told her how Richard had put up with years of my mental problems, which she still thought were totally fabricated, something I was just milking for sympathy.

My therapist wasn't having any of it. "He hit her. Look at her leg. She did exactly what she should have done, what I would have told her to do."

This calmed my mom down a little, who, at least in front of the therapist, was willing to concede that this wasn't entirely my fault. She called my dad and explained what was going on. He wanted to talk now, so we made plans to meet in a store parking lot a few miles down the road, between my therapist's office and his work.

My dad was waiting when we got there with the kids. He didn't seem as angry as my mother, just shocked and disappointed.

"Julie, what did you do?" he asked, sounding tired and exasperated.

I tried to explain how things had gotten so out of hand. I told him how the doctor had seen my bruise and forced me to report it to the police. I told him that I had only meant to document the incident, just as we had tried to document Richard's affair, and that it was never my intention to have him arrested. That I had begged the police not to do so. None of it was supposed to go down like this, but my hand had been forced the whole way.

It was what it was, so there wasn't much for him to say. We just had to wait and see. The kids were getting restless and starting to whine, so my mom said we should head back. My dad still had work, so he peeled off on his own while we took the kids home.

Back at the house, my mother was in such a foul mood that I had to ask her to leave, as she was adding exponentially to the stress I was already experiencing. She left and then it was just me and the kids.

I tried to explain the situation to them in the gentlest of terms, informing them that daddy had gotten into some trouble and wouldn't be coming home for a little while. Were they sad?

On the contrary, they jumped up and held hands and started circling me and singing, doing a little dance. They were thrilled he wouldn't be coming home. It was understandable, given how Richard had treated them. It was difficult for me to be quite so sanguine, sitting there waiting for the other shoe to fall.

Eventually, the police officer from earlier called to let me know they had picked up Richard and booked him into jail but that he was already out on bond. He was supposed to be going to his grandparents' house, as he was barred from coming back to the house tonight. They had scheduled a court hearing for me in the morning to set up a protective order.

"I should tell you also, your dad is an asshole," the officer added before letting me off the phone.

Apparently, my dad had called the police station and told them that they had the wrong person—it was *me* they should have arrested, not Richard.

I would later find out that Richard had used his one phone call to contact my father from jail and accused me of making everything up. The bruise? I must have done it to myself to frame him. I was off my rocker, crazy, clearly belonged back at the mental hospital.

Never mind that none of this made much sense or that my father knew Richard was having an affair and capable of lying— my dad still believed him over me, or sided with him, at any rate.

For their part, the police didn't buy any of this. The officer told me Richard had changed his story repeatedly during questioning and was obviously lying.

"We believe you," the officer said over the phone. "But you should know what your dad told us."

That night was terrible. I was worried that Richard would show up at the house at any minute. The police had offered to check in on the house, driving by to make sure everything was in order, but it wasn't like they could stand guard all night. I didn't feel safe there at all, not with Richard out there surely plotting his revenge.

Later that night, my phone buzzed with a text message. It was Eric again, asking if I was okay and saying he "just knew" that something bad had happened. I texted back to ask how he could possibly know that, to which he simply responded that it was just a feeling he had, an intuition, some kind of premonition telling him to check on me.

He also said that whatever it was, there was no need to face it alone—he could be there, if I wanted. I was feeling so vulnerable all on my own in that house that his showing up out of the blue to offer support, to stand in my corner, really did seem like he was some guardian angel sent down to watch over me.

This was, of course, exactly what he wanted me to believe.

FOURTEEN

THE REAL ERIC

The next morning, I appeared in court for my hearing. The city appointed me a lawyer, free of charge, who sat and listened to me tell my life story. I told her almost everything about Richard and his behavior toward me, information I hadn't ever uttered to another soul. Completely appalled by the sordid details, she wanted to go all in against him, not just for the kick, but for everything, all of his abuse.

This was terrifying to me. I had just told her how he would urinate on me, how he tied me to him at night—all these insane, cruel things I had allowed him to do to me over the years. Part of my resistance to going after Richard for his years of abuse was my fear of reprisal, but I was also so ashamed of allowing him to treat me that way. I felt complicit in it, just as I had felt complicit in what my father had done to me. When you let someone abuse you for so long, you start to feel responsible for letting it happen.

I begged her not to include any of the history in her statement. She agreed and only told the judge about the kick, which was enough to get him to issue a protective order. Richard was no longer allowed back onto the property or within a thousand feet of me.

The court order meant nothing to him, though, and he started violating it right away. That very night, he drove by my house with his headlights off and parked right out front. Peeping through a crack in the blinds, I watched him just sitting there in his car, watching the house. This was terrifying, as he kept guns in the back of the car. A slip of paper from the city couldn't keep him from marching up the driveway and kicking in the door if he really wanted.

I called the police, but Richard took off before they arrived. He just wanted me to know that the protective order could not keep me safe. The police again offered to drive by the house regularly, but I still didn't feel safe.

This is why I decided to turn to Eric for help. He started coming by in the evenings to stand guard by the window in case Richard showed up. I couldn't have been more thankful. He was like a godsend, truly a guardian angel.

Though Richard must have seen the truck out front and Eric sitting by the window, he was undeterred. He called me a few days later, in open violation of the protective order, and told me he intended to get revenge and wouldn't stop until "every last drop of [my] blood was spilt."

Since he continued to violate the protective order, I went to the police to see what else could be done. I regretted preventing the lawyer from including his history of abusing me in the court records. When I told the police that he had been raping me, they advised against upping the charges against him. They said accusing my own husband of rape would just make me "look like a man hater." They clearly didn't take the allegations seriously at all.

Certain the police couldn't keep me safe, I relied on Eric more and more. He was being so kind by coming over at night to stand guard, protecting us, even helping to take care of the kids. I never left them alone with him, as it was impossible for me to trust men when it came to their safety, but he helped me put them to bed. He was quickly becoming a small part of our lives.

There were warning signs, though, of course, red flags that I should have taken seriously. I was in the bathroom one day, crying hysterically about my life unraveling before me, when Eric started knocking on the door. When I wouldn't open up, he kicked the door down. At the time, I took it as a sign of concern, ignoring how violent and aggressive this was.

I would soon find out just how violent he could be.

BETRAYAL

The next two weeks flew by, fast and furious. I was working with lawyers and the police to figure out the situation with

Richard, getting all my ducks in a row. I was going to need to file for divorce and start working toward collecting child support and any alimony due. It was all happening so fast that I was in a daze most of the time, but it was also exciting. On one hand, my life was unraveling, but on the other it seemed to finally be starting. I was finally breaking free from Richard. It was a struggle, but it was also an opportunity to start living for real.

All of that changed one day when Eric wanted me to go with him to his sister's house to grab something. Though we had been spending a lot of time together, I was hesitant to go out into the world with him. Richard and I were still technically married, and he could accuse me of having "an affair" with Eric, even though we were just friends, to fight me in the coming custody battle. He had been coming by trying to take pictures and collect evidence of another man in the house. I felt a lot of guilt over this too, but I told myself it was fine. Eric was only a friend, and I was allowed to have friends.

Eric convinced me to go with him by saying I needed a break from everything that was going on with Richard and should just get out of the house for a bit. He helped me into his truck and drove to his sister's house.

His sister was standoffish and kind of rude, which I later learned was because she "didn't like white girls." When Eric asked me to go upstairs with him to get something, I obliged just to get away from her.

I followed Eric upstairs but stopped in the hallway when he went into a bedroom. Something felt wrong and I didn't want to go into a bedroom with another man, even a friend, but he waved me in. Not wanting to upset him, I followed.

As soon as I was inside, he slammed the door shut and blocked it with his body. Then, for the first time, but certainly not the last, he raped me, violently. In a moment, he had transformed into a whole different person.

Lying in the bed afterward, staring up at the ceiling, I tried to comprehend what had just transpired. Though I had tried to stop him, had said no, I did not view the assault as rape. In my mind, I had spent all this time with him, and now that he had taken it to a physical place...we must have accidentally slipped into a relationship of some kind. *Look what you did*, the voice in my head said accusatorially. I was so mad at myself for letting it happen. I was terrified of the judge finding out about this and losing the custody battle with Richard.

Things were never the same with Eric again. It was like a switch had been thrown and he transformed from good to evil. He was suddenly tyrannical and controlling. He was no longer the pro-tector but now the boss, and I had to do whatever he said, *or else.*

Shucking off Richard only to fall into Eric's hands was like going straight from the frying pan down into the bowels of hell. Eric was far more violent than Richard had ever been. And he now had far more leverage over me than Richard ever had. Over the last few weeks, he had learned about my hopes, my fears, and my vulnerabilities, all of which he started to use against me. He threatened to tell Richard about "my affair" with him so that I would lose my kids.

He had complete and total control over me. So when the weekend rolled around and Eric wanted me to accompany him on a trip, I didn't have much say in the matter. He had some business in California and wanted me to ride along. Just as he had convinced me to go to his sister's house, he told me that getting out of town and away from the nastiness with Richard would be good for me. I didn't trust him much at this point, but I knew I had little say in the matter. He wouldn't accept a refusal. I told him I wasn't interested, but he just kept pushing, refusing to take no for an answer.

His tone was almost sweet as he kept repeating that it would be good for me, it would be good for me. He was trying to maintain his role as my protector and steward, as abusers often do to keep things progressing. They keep showing you a little bit of kindness even as the abuse escalates, stringing you along as they lay the snare. Eric needed me to believe that he was the only one who could keep me safe from Richard. He was the new boyfriend, here to save me from the last. This was an appealing narrative, as it was easier to accept that we were in some kind of relationship than to accept the truth—that it was rape, and I had fallen straight back into another abusive dynamic.

I eventually agreed to go on the condition that I could bring my dog, Alex, along with us. Eric resisted at first, as he didn't like dogs and didn't want one in the truck, but he eventually relented. This made me feel more comfortable with going since Alex was a big black Lab that made me feel safer, though I was soon to be disabused of this notion.

I started making plans to go. Richard had won visitation rights and had the kids every other weekend. My parents could also help watch them since they knew I was struggling, and while they didn't want to step up and help, they were supportive of their grandkids. This meant I had somewhere safe to take my kids when I lied and told my parents I was going to Vegas with some girlfriends, since I didn't want them to know about Eric and our so-called relationship.

THE TRIP

That Friday morning, Eric came by the house in his semitruck to pick me up. Though surprised to see no trailer attached, since this was ostensibly a work trip and he was a long-haul trucker, I didn't question him because I didn't know the business. I certainly had no way of knowing he didn't need a trailer because the cargo was me. I had my apprehensions about the trip, but I in no way suspected that Eric was the monster he turned out to be.

Alex went into the back of the sleeper cab, stretching out on the mattress, and I rode up front with Eric. We stopped at a Peruvian restaurant in Salt Lake City, where he introduced me to some of his national cuisine, which seemed nice and normal enough. I was still on edge, though, wondering if I was making a huge mistake coming along.

After eating, we headed out and drove all the way to the California coast, ten hours straight, only stopping for gas and restroom breaks. We arrived in Huntington Beach and spent an uneventful night in a hotel.

The next morning, Eric parked the truck in a lot at the beach. He wanted to go down to the sand and walk along the docks, but first he wanted me to get changed into a different shirt. He took out a shirt with Little Miss Sunshine and a cartoon character printed across the front. I looked at the shirt with mild disgust, realizing it was probably his daughter's shirt. The thing was tiny and clearly made for children. It wasn't flattering to be told it reminded him of me.

I took the shirt and feigned gratitude, planning to bury it in my bag, but Eric wanted me to put it on so he could take pictures of me down by the water. This seemed strange, but not worth fighting over; it was just a shirt. I changed into the shirt and followed him down to the beach.

Eric held the dog while I posed by the water. The whole episode was really embarrassing, and I couldn't help but think what the people on the beach thought of me with this man snapping pictures of me in a child's shirt.

Afterward, we walked the boardwalk and hung out on the beach for a few hours. I convinced myself that maybe things weren't so bad after all. Maybe this was just a lighthearted getaway after all, and my worries were for nothing. Other than the stupid shirt, everything seemed relatively normal.

Eric went back to the truck with Alex to take a nap while I stayed at the shore. When he came back a few hours later, with the sun already going down, he said we needed to get going.

He had a meeting for work later, and we would need to drive through the night to make it on time. A business meeting in the dead of night seemed odd, but he was a long-haul trucker after all, so what did I know?

We got back into the truck and headed out. At several weigh stations along the way, we had to stop so that Eric could show his driver logs. He asked me to doctor them to make it look like he hadn't been driving as much as he had since he was well over the legal limit. It felt wrong, but I acceded. Talking to the uniformed men at the weigh stations made me feel safer and alleviated some of my anxiety about the whole trip. When we stopped for food and gas, Eric took me in with him, and again everything seemed pretty normal.

Things started to get weird a little farther down the road, when all of a sudden Eric said he had forgotten he wasn't allowed to have passengers in the truck.

"What?" I said.

"I can't have passengers when I'm working," he said. "You can't be here."

"You're just remembering this now?"

There was apparently some checkpoint ahead, so Eric needed me to hide where no one could see me. He pulled the truck over and had me get down on the mattress in the back so he could cover me up with blankets, loose clothing lying around, his duffel bag, the dog, trash off the floorboard, anything he could find.

The truck started moving again. Lying flat on my stomach with this pile of stuff over me, I started to panic. Eric insisted we would get in trouble if anyone saw me—not just him, but me too. I didn't know what he was talking about, but I was obviously afraid of getting into legal trouble in the middle of my custody battle with Richard. I was kicking myself for letting him talk me into coming, but he promised it would be fine if I just sat still and kept quiet. He claimed he would talk our way out of whatever trouble we were in.

The longer he had me hidden in the back, the more scared I got. He was now hiding me from the men in uniform who had kept me feeling safe. Suddenly, they were the enemy. It was also hard to breathe underneath all the detritus, and I had to dig out some space in front of my face to get a little air.

When the truck came to a stop, I peered out of my little air tunnel to see big overhead lights, white and as bright as daylight, shining down on us. I heard men's voices that sounded like they were outside, somewhat muffled by the pile of clothes and blankets on top of me. It was very busy. The truck kept lurching as we moved through the line, and I felt the whole cab tremble when someone hopped aboard and started speaking to Eric in Spanish. Eric answered questions—I had no idea what he was saying—and eventually the truck shook again as whoever had come aboard climbed back down. The truck started to move, and we pulled off.

At the time, it never even occurred to me that we were crossing an international border. I thought we were still somewhere in California. I had no reason to think we would be crossing over into Mexico, as Eric had given me no indication of this.

He had me ride covered up and hidden until we were miles and miles from the checkpoint, but eventually he hollered into the back that it was safe to come out now. He didn't want me coming back up into the front, though, saying it was better if I stayed back just in case. In case of what? I had no idea.

We drove a few more hours before Eric had his next surprise realization. This time it was that we couldn't have a dog where we were headed. Even though he had been fine with Alex before, suddenly he was a big liability. He told me we were going to have to leave Alex behind. I refused—if he goes, I go. Eric rejected this, but I wouldn't let up. He threatened to throw Alex out the window. I panicked and pleaded with him to be reasonable, now just sobbing.

Eric suddenly remembered—or so he said—a friend in town with a fenced yard. He suggested that maybe we could leave Alex there while we went wherever it was that we were going. I said, "Yes, please, call him!" Eric phoned his friend. They started conversing in Spanish, so I couldn't understand a word of it. I kept asking what was happening, would it be okay? Eric ignored me, so all I could do was hope and pray this friend would come through for me.

"Is it okay?" I asked.

Eric tossed me the phone. "I don't know. Here, you work it out."

I looked down at the phone, confused. "Can he stay there or not?"

"Ask him yourself," Eric said with a cruel smirk.

I put the phone to my ear and tried to make my case, but the person on the other end of the line clearly couldn't speak

English. Speaking slowly, as if this would somehow magically render me comprehensible, I tried to make arrangements for Alex. I struggled with the words, wishing there was some way to make him understand.

When I started sobbing, the man on the phone started laughing at me. Then Eric started laughing too, and it was clear that this was all one big joke for them, with me the butt of it. I gave the phone back to Eric and got into the back with Alex, just holding him for comfort.

Eric kept driving while I kept quiet in the back. He hadn't thrown Alex out of the truck, at least not yet, so it seemed best to avoid the subject of the dog altogether.

Eric stopped at a Spanish restaurant for food. By now, the mood had completely shifted, and Eric was cruel and domineering again, not at all like he had been earlier at the beach. He told me I was coming in with him to eat and Alex was staying in the truck. Even that was a relief, as I was still worried he would just throw Alex out.

The restaurant menus were all in Spanish, the signs were in Spanish, and everyone was speaking Spanish. I was the only white person around, and while there are areas of Southern California like this, this seemed unusual. It started to dawn on me that he had taken me over the border, out of the country, without telling me.

Eric ordered himself an entire fish, but nothing for me. The fish looked to have been plucked straight out of the water and grilled whole, head on, which was something I hadn't seen before. Eric offered me an eye, and when I declined, he plucked one out and ate it right in front of me, trying to gross me out.

Eric took his sweet time eating, and I was getting worried about Alex being alone in the truck. He had separation anxiety, and I was concerned that he would try to get out. I repeatedly asked Eric if I could go check on him, but he kept refusing. When he finally consented, he followed me outside.

I went back to the truck and opened the door. Alex came bounding out, and I could see that he had chewed through the driver's side seat belt, which was just hanging. Eric went absolutely crazy when he saw it. He started screaming at the dog and kicking at him while I tried to get between them, explaining that he has anxiety.

"I don't care about his anxiety!" Eric shouted. "We have somewhere to be. Look what he did to the truck."

Eric found a thick cargo strap and used it to bind Alex's jaw shut. He then tied him down to the back of the truck and ushered me back inside. Not knowing what to do, I petted Alex and then followed Eric back inside. I was worried about the dog the whole time Eric was eating, knowing he wasn't just going to lie there by himself all tied up like that.

By the time Eric finally finished eating, Alex had broken free but was still waiting for me by the truck. Eric flipped out again, this time kicking Alex in the ribs and whipping him with the strap. Alex was yelping and wailing, trying to get away. When I tried to get between them, Eric raised the strap—as if to use it on me—but two men passing by started shouting at Eric.

Eric sized them up and proceeded to get into a verbal altercation. They were all speaking Spanish, but it was clear the guys were trying to get Eric to calm down and he was telling them to mind their own business. When they wouldn't leave, Eric finally lowered the strap and shooed me away. I went to check on Alex, to make sure he was okay. The guys wandered off, kind of keeping an eye on the situation, and Eric told me to get in the truck. I took Alex into the back with me, and we pulled away. The whole scene was horrible, but I was so thankful those two guys interfered, as it could have been much worse.

We drove for a while longer, with Eric yelling at me the whole time. He was screaming that we weren't going to be able to pass inspection checkpoints with his seat belt in tatters, and he blamed it all on me and my dumb dog. I just sat there in the back, holding Alex and crying hysterically at this point. I had no idea what to do.

When we arrived at a small blue motel later, the situation with Alex still hadn't been resolved. Eric seemed to have forgotten about it for now, which was for the best, in my mind. Instead of going into the motel, Eric parked nearby and took out some pills he wanted me to take. I told him I didn't want any, to which he said he didn't care. He crushed up one of the pills and poured the powder into a protein shake. He gave the bottle a good shake and handed it to me.

When I repeated that I didn't want any, he started screaming at me to drink it. Given what had just happened with the dog, this was scary enough that I just gave in and took my chances with the drugs—anything to get him to calm down. I was worried about what he might do to Alex if I didn't comply.

Eric then said we needed to hide the truck, why or from whom I had no idea, but he pulled around the block and parked in an alley. He told me to come up front. Whatever drugs he had given me were already starting to hit, and I felt so nauseated that I could barely manage to crawl up front.

Eric then proceeded to rape me again, even more aggressively and violently than last time, only this time my body could barely even move or respond. I was crying again, and even that felt difficult; my body was so detached that it could barely even execute autonomous functions.

Afterward, he got out of the truck and came around to my side. When he opened the door, I tumbled out, leaden and practically lifeless, right into his arms. Eric knew he couldn't walk me into the motel in this state, so he had to sneak me in. He put a jacket over my head, which made it hard to see anything. It hardly mattered because I couldn't walk anyway. I had to lean on him for support.

Eric then walked me out of the alley and back to the motel, around the office, and to the rooms in the back. He produced a key somehow. I wasn't sure if he had one in advance or if I had blacked out while he had gone in and paid. This was certainly possible, as I was fading in and out of consciousness even then.

DOG MAN

The next thing I remember was waking up in the shower with Eric shaving my whole body, which was dehumanizing in the extreme, but I felt too sick to resist. Though I might have been hallucinating, I saw two bottles of hair dye on the shelf, the exact same ones my mom used to have, and I was horrified at the prospect of him dyeing my hair, which underscored my sense of helplessness and loss of agency.

I continued to float in and out of consciousness throughout the night, blackness and empty time interspersed with scenes of horror. I woke up in bed with Eric laughing at me, mockingly asking whether I had a headache, which of course had been caused by whatever he had given me. My body needed to vomit, to expel the drugs, but he kept warning me that I had better not throw up, so I held it in as best as I could.

The next thing I knew, someone else was in the room and climbing on top of me. Absolutely horrified, I looked around for Eric, momentarily feeling a sense of relief to see him by the side of the bed, as if he was going to save me from this stranger. My fear returned when I saw him taking pictures. Eric wasn't going to save me from the other man—they were in on this together.

The man on top of me was speaking in Spanish, and while I didn't understand any of it, I could tell he was being lewd and nasty. He placed a baton between my knees to keep my legs pried open while he raped me. Spit kept flying from his mouth, hanging from his mustache, so I turned my head away. That is when I noticed a pistol lying on the side of the bed, which made my heart jump with fear. I had no idea whether they planned to kill me after this.

This went on for a while, this disgusting man raping me as Eric snapped photos. The man kept talking, calling me names, and suddenly it occurred to me who he was—this was *Dog Man*. It was the person on the phone earlier who was supposed to watch Alex. Eric was letting his friend rape me.

Eventually, I regained consciousness, alone now. The blinds were pulled shut, so there was no way to know whether it was day or night, to track how long I had been in bed. My head felt like it was going to crack open from the worst migraine of my entire life. Someone was moving in the bathroom, and I was actually relieved when Eric stepped out, not Dog Man, which was the saddest thing I could imagine.

HOMEWARD BOUND

The next morning, we packed our things and went back to the truck, where Alex was sitting in the back, alive and safe. I had no idea how he got there, whether he had really stayed with Dog Man or had been in the truck the whole time. I didn't care; I was just happy to see him safe. I laid down in the back and put my arms around him while Eric started the truck.

Eric snuck us back over the border and took me back home to Utah. I worried about what the neighbors might think when he dropped me off at the house. Richard had printed and made copies of my medical files and handed them out to all the neighbors, telling them that I was off my rocker and that he needed them to keep an eye on me. When I got home, I felt physically tainted, as if any onlooker would be able to see what had happened to me just by looking at me. I didn't see anyone, so I hurried inside and closed the door behind me.

Absolutely exhausted, I went right to bed and slept for twelve hours straight, the sleep of the dead.

In the morning, I headed straight to the dog shelter and surrendered Alex into their custody. It had been foolish to think he could protect me from Eric. To the contrary, I had had no way to protect Alex and still didn't. He was one more liability that Eric could use against me. I wasn't going to put his life at risk like that, not again. I couldn't save myself, but at least I could save the dog.

FIFTEEN

THE ABNORMAL LIFE

y kids weren't coming home until the next day, so I had a little time to collect myself after the trip. Being back in the house after everything I had been through was surreal. The whole world felt hazy, like a dream. When my kids came home, I had to switch back into mom mode: chipper and caring, saying hello to the kids and telling them that I loved them, but I was just going through the motions. Putting on a smile like everything was okay was so utterly false that the whole world felt fake. Nothing about my life felt real or normal after the nightmare world I had come home from. Everything felt deceptive, even the fabric of reality and the passage of time.

My mind was already starting to dissociate at this point. The trip had disabused me of any pretense of being in a normal relationship with Eric. I had tried to convince myself that he just liked the idea of "sharing" me with other people, that it was some gross kink, but I wasn't able to maintain this delusion on the way back from California.

The only defense mechanism I had left was compartmentalization, sectioning off what happened to me and cordoning it to some other part of my life. That thing with Eric, that happened over there, in that other life, and it had nothing to do with me here and now with my kids. Thinking this way was the only way to make it through the day, but I couldn't cordon it off fully, and the horror of that weekend experience was starting to actively distress me again.

There was no compartmentalizing Eric himself, though. He was still in my life and could show up at the house at any moment. He didn't appear right away, at least not for a couple of days, though he texted and called throughout. He was very much present, especially in my head. Richard was out of the picture, at least for now. He was trying to stay away from the house now that we were locked in a custody battle, but Eric was here—and so much worse.

He showed up at the house later in the week to let me know there would be more trips like the last one, and that I should be ready. He wanted to go out again that very next weekend.

"What do you mean, another trip?" I asked fearfully. "Like last time?"

"Yeah, another trip," he said, and the laughter in his eyes made it clear that he took great pleasure from torturing me this way.

"You want to share me again?" I asked, my voice already cracking.

Eric laughed, as he thought my phrasing was really funny. "Yeah, I want to *share you* again."

I broke down and started crying, begging him, please, no, anything but that. I still didn't quite understand what was going on, but if it was more of the same, I would rather be dead. But, of course, there was no saying no. No negotiating. Eric reminded me of the pictures he had taken and again threatened to send them to Richard to use against me in the custody battle. He said now everyone would know the truth: that I was a prostitute.

When he told me there would be more trips and I made it clear I didn't want to go, he became angry and put both hands around my neck, choking me. I fell to the floor, and he leaned in with all his weight on my neck. I was panicking, clawing at his hands...but he would not let go. He said that he could kill me if he wanted to and that someday, he *would* be the one to kill me. I believed him. Why wouldn't I?

Life was now even more of a living hell. For the next five months, Eric took me away almost every weekend to use my body and sell it to other men.

Coming home during the week, things were not much better. Trying to maintain a normal life was impossible. I continued to work at the preschool during the week. There were my kids to take care of. I had the ongoing custody battle with Richard. I was also volunteering at the kids' school and working with the PTA. The whole time, I was traumatized, desperately just trying to hold it all together. I was living a double life as a PTA mom during the week and a sex slave on the weekends.

I did everything I could to hide what was happening to me, to maintain the illusion of normalcy. I didn't want to lose custody of my kids forever or have everyone find out what was happening to me. I didn't want to go to jail for prostitution, which Eric insisted would happen.

He was forcing me to commit other crimes as well. He drove me to his workplace one night in the semitruck. We parked just off premises and crawled through a hidden hole in the fencing. Once inside, he started going through the other trucks, stealing tools and personal items from them. He took a mattress from the back of one of the trucks to replace the cheap, thin, dirty one he had in his. I had to help him carry all the loot back to his truck. I hated doing this, but I felt I had no choice but to be his accomplice.

Knowing I still had a key to the preschool, Eric wanted me to break in and steal money and items from the school. Here I stood my ground, refusing to double-cross Teresa in this way, ever. We were in line at the bank when I flat out refused, and I was glad we were because he looked ready to backhand me on the spot if there hadn't been people and security all around. The next time I was back at the house alone, I threw out the key to the preschool so that he would stop asking.

HORROR AT HOME

I was utterly exhausted, and my poor mental health was further taxed by Eric's abuse. I tried to cope by turning to self-harm: I started cutting myself again, both as a release and a punishment for getting myself into this situation. Eric saw the fresh scars and got angry at me for "marking myself" and lowering my market value. He forbade me from cutting myself and threatened to tell Richard about any self-harm, as it would make me present as too unstable to be a parent.

Without cutting as an option, I was forced to rely on compartmentalization as my only crutch, trying to confine this hell with Eric to my time with him. I tried to keep Eric out of my thoughts. There was nothing I could do about him dragging me along on his trips, but I could try not to think about them when I was home. Even if he owned my body, he didn't own my mind.

Although my childhood experiences had made me quite good at compartmentalizing abuse, keeping Eric separate from my daily life wasn't possible when he was around literally all the time. He had forced himself into my life and was now bringing all these crazy, depraved people right up to my front door with him. There was nothing I could do about it; there was no way to keep my two lives separate.

Eric was over at the house when his wife, who he claimed was his ex-wife, came knocking on my door in the middle of the night. He peeked out the window and spotted her car outside.

"Don't answer," he said. "It's just Sharon."

I shooed him off, as this was just Sharon, who I knew from the preschool. What was the big deal? This transpired when I was still confused about the nature of my relationship with Eric, shortly after he raped me but before our first trip together. I answered the door and Sharon burst into the house, going off on me in Spanish. I tried to calm her down, sitting her down on the couch and getting her something to drink. Eric had left the room but came back in and slunk down on the sofa next to her. They started arguing with each other, and I had no idea what was going on, but she was clearly upset that he was with me.

"What's the problem?" I asked, trying to defuse the situation. "You all are divorced, right?"

She looked over at Eric, then back at me. "Yeah, yeah. Divorced. *Divorced*," she said, as if she just remembered, trying to hide her anger.

Eric must have been coaching her on what to say. I later found out that they were still married. She clearly knew more than what she was letting on at the time, even if she was jealous about my so-called relationship with Eric.

They talked more, and Sharon eventually got up to leave. I followed Eric outside onto the porch to watch her go. She got in her car, but instead of backing out of the driveway, she floored the gas pedal and tore across the front lawn as if she were aiming for us. I hurriedly took cover, but she stopped just short of the porch; otherwise, she would have definitely hit us.

As time went on, Eric kept inserting himself further and further into my real life, causing me more and more difficulties. I was at the kids' school one day and saw topless photos of me on all the cars, tucked under windshield wipers and into windows. I ran around the parking lot before the bell rang trying to collect them, but parents started coming out before I could get to them all. Nobody ever said anything to me about it—because they were too polite or too scandalized, I'll never know—but it was humiliating and horrible, nonetheless.

Eric also sent compromising photos of me to Richard. I got an email from Richard on Christmas Day, forwarding pictures of me with other men, as if I were having sex with them and not being raped. Richard claimed not to know who had sent them, just saying I should figure out what was up, but I think he wanted me to know that Eric was in touch with him.

The two of them started collaborating to terrorize me. Eric actually testified on Richard's behalf in my domestic violence case against him and also helped him win full custody of my kids. They used pictures Eric had taken to advertise me to make the case that I was unfit to be a mother when I was "sleeping around" so much.

Thinking I could maintain a normal life and function as a normal mother had clearly been a pipe dream. I couldn't keep this secret life separate from my "real" life because this was my real life now.

Richard ultimately did win full custody of the kids that January because I didn't show up at the hearing. I had a terrible choice to make. Eric had started acting more comfortable around my daughter, Kaylee, wanting to hold her all the time and kissing her on the lips. It had become clear that my home could never again be safe—not for me, and certainly not for the kids.

I surrendered custody of them to Richard in January 2009 to keep them safe from Eric. Since they needed a place to live, I also let Richard take over the house, which was fine by him, of course. He had been living with his grandparents during our separation. I was relieved to have my kids safe and in the house, even if I had to leave. They would never be safe there with me living in the house—at least not while Eric walked free. During this time in my life, I completely forgot that Eric no longer had my kids as leverage over me. I had been permitting him to subject me to so much abuse, for so long now, I could no longer see any way out.

Eric found an apartment for me twenty miles away, in another part of town. The divorce from Richard wouldn't be finalized until March, but I was living by myself in this new apartment. I didn't even remember getting the place, as Eric had given me a pill that put me in a daze for several days straight. When I came to, I was in this strange apartment, which was apparently mine. The lease was in both of our names. I was surprised he put his real name on the lease, but he did. It was horrifying seeing a lease with both of us on it, as if I were his wife or something.

The apartment was mine in name only, however. He was paying the rent. We never discussed the matter, but it was understood to be part of my "work package." As long as he was trafficking me and selling me to other men, the apartment was mine to stay in. This was an unstated arrangement and not one I entered into freely, but I accepted it because I needed a place to live.

Eric kept a key, of course, and came and went as he pleased. He kept a pair of jeans and a bottle of cologne there, and he often came over at night to torment or rape me. I even had to allow another man in the house once.

This happened not long after I woke up in the back seat of a strange car, my body still locked in paralysis from the drugs they had given me. I could barely move my head, which was banging against the window with every bump in the road. We were driving through the desert, with the full moon shining overhead as the only real source of light, basically riding down a beaten path. There were no signs or road markers, and I had no idea how they were navigating out there in the middle of nowhere.

My whole body hurt, my head too, and I just wanted to find a ditch to vomit and die in. I was already in hell, so literal hell was preferable. The car jostled me and shifted my weight, rolling my head to the side, which is when I saw two other sets of knees next to mine. There were two other girls in the car, and they were literally *girls*, just two Hispanic teenagers. I avoided making eye contact, as I felt powerless to help them, which was a terrible feeling that still haunts me today.

Eric was in the passenger seat, and the driver was a woman with curly hair and a raspy voice. It took me a minute to recognize her as his sister, which came as a shock. How much did she know about him and what he was doing? Clearly, she knew quite a lot if she was taxiing three drugged women through the backcountry in the middle of the night. I could hardly believe a woman could do such a thing to another woman.

We came to a stucco building so run-down and dusty that the walls looked like they were made of old concrete. The windows were all boarded up, and the whole place looked condemned. Eric got out and was rummaging around in the trunk for his maroon duffel bag. He came around to my side of the car with the bag slung over his shoulder and opened the door. I fell out of the car. He tried to help me stand, but my legs were like Jell-O. He walked me into the building while his sister shepherded the two young girls around the side of the house, to where I didn't know.

The floors inside were so dirty I couldn't tell if they were floors at all or just dirt. There was trash everywhere: crumpled papers and bags, cigarette butts ground out on the floor, heaps of refuse swept up against the wall and just left there. The place was not fit for a dog, and it was unclear whether anyone did live here. There didn't seem to be any electricity, so it was dark inside.

Someone emerged from the arched doorway of a hallway leading into the darkness in the back. It took me a moment to recognize him—it was Dog Man. He gave Eric a big hug and they spoke in Spanish lightheartedly, as if this were all the most natural thing in the world.

At the sound of their voices, someone else came into the room, a Hispanic kid. He looked barely legal, if he was at all, just a teenager.

Eric shoved me toward Dog Man to be propped up so that he could rummage through the duffel bag. He pulled out an envelope full of money and a couple of bags of drugs, which he laid on the windowsill, presumably for later, for whom exactly I couldn't know.

Eric then turned to me and motioned at the boy. "I want you to take good care of my cousin."

Dog Man led me and this boy, the supposed cousin, through the arched alleyway and down a dark corridor. I was terrified to leave Eric. As bad as he was, he was still a known entity, and there was safety in that. Dog Man and this strange boy were not, and I had no idea what they had planned. But I was too out of it to even protest, so I just let them lead me into the back.

We passed by several dark rooms where I could hear the sound of men having sex, presumably raping the two girls who had been in the back with me. I realized we were in some kind of illegal brothel. This was horrifying, but there was no way to help and nowhere to run. They took me into a small room with no windows, deep in the bowels of the building. There was nothing in there except a couple of dirty old mattresses on the floor and a piece of fencing that I mistook for a headboard until I saw dozens of zip ties and fabric restraints hanging from the boards.

Dog Man told me to lie down on one of the mattresses, but I didn't want to because it was absolutely filthy. At that moment, all my feelings of disgust were focused on the mattress. I didn't have a choice, though, so I did what he said. I could still hardly stand.

Dog Man started trying to zip-tie my wrists to the boards, which sent me into panic mode. I started to struggle and squirm.

"Are you going to make this harder for me?" he demanded, screaming in my face, speaking English suddenly for the first time, which came as a shock. "Do what I say, or this could get much worse!"

I tried to force my body to go limp, but it just wouldn't. He started pulling on my wrist, bending it down toward my forearm, and it felt like he was trying to break my arm. It was only the pain that forced me to realize that I was still fighting him. I did everything I could to make my muscles relax.

When Dog Man finally had me bound to the fencing, he lit a candle in the corner of the room and started having his way with me. When he was done, he turned to the cousin as if to say, *your turn*. The cousin seemed hesitant, shy about it even, but Dog Man kept egging him on, pushing him toward me, until finally the cousin gave in and went through with it.

Dog Man stood over us taking pictures the whole time, which I was used to at this point but still found sickening. I tried to keep my head turned to the side, avoiding the camera but also the gaze of this young boy. When I did see his face, this young innocent face, I wondered what had gone so wrong in his life that he could do this to me. They both knew it was wrong; you could see it in this kid's guilty hesitation just as clearly as you could see it in Dog Man's sadistic grin.

I just couldn't understand it. So much had gone wrong in my life to bring me to this point, which was a story I knew and would eventually come to understand. I couldn't fathom what had gone so wrong in their lives that they could torture another human being like this. It made no sense, and it still makes no sense to me.

Part of me kept hoping Eric would come back, even if he started raping me too. More than whatever they were subjecting me to, I was afraid of being left with them permanently. *Is this my new home? Is this where I live? Is this my life now?*

I must have passed out a second time because the next thing I knew, Eric was helping me into a pickup truck. It was a relief to see him, a relief to be leaving, until I realized this wasn't the car we had come in. The sister was gone. They were loading me into a pickup. In horror, I realized that Dog Man was at the wheel and the cousin was in the back. Eric loaded me into the back with his cousin before getting in himself. I had to ride smooshed between the two of them. So repulsed by this kid who had just done this terrible thing to me, I leaned into Eric, the man who had let him. It was a confusing feeling, but one I had become accustomed to by now: leaning into my trafficker out of fear of the men he was foisting on me.

We drove through the desert until we came to a parking lot where Eric had left his semitruck. I was practically relieved to see the truck and couldn't wait to get into the back, safe on my mattress. To my continued horror, the cousin got in the truck with us.

I went into the back and pulled the curtain shut while they rode up front. *Why is he still here?* I wanted to leave him back there in the desert forever. I kept hoping we would drop him off somewhere, but we never did. Eric brought him back to the apartment he'd set up for me, as I no longer had the house. He told me to "take care" of him.

I spent three days living with my rapist in the apartment Eric had secured for me. This boy slept in my bed, ate from my fridge, went through my things, and continued to rape me the whole time. It was horrifying.

My "reward" for taking such good care of him was Eric taking us swimming at the rec center. I didn't want to be there, of course, and I wasn't allowed to swim by myself. I had to sit with Eric in the hot tub, with his arm around me, the whole time. The only time he let me get up was to help some young kid to the waterslide, but when I came back, Eric accused me of flirting with this random little kid.

He was angry, yelling again, telling me he was going to punish me. This was my life now, and I couldn't escape it, couldn't even leave it behind on our trips; Eric wasn't going to allow it. My life belonged to him now, and he wasn't ever going to let me forget it.

SIXTEEN

A DIFFICULT RECOVERY

Years later, having finally wrested my life and my freedom away from Eric, I can hardly comprehend how I survived the years of unending nightmare of abuse—beginning with my father, then Richard, and finally Eric. Overcoming my history of abusive relationships with the men in my life was excruciatingly difficult, even after Barry helped me break free from Eric. Although being forced to negotiate a truck deal with Barry was a significant source of stress at the time, it was clearly divine providence. Eric effectively handed me over to Barry—miraculously, a good man who helped me with each and every step of the long, arduous process of getting my life back on track.

We started dating in the midst of some truly bad times. I was dealing with my divorce, the custody battle, and Eric stalking me, but Barry was there for me throughout. Four months after beginning to date, we got married in June. This helped me win back partial custody of the kids. We were able to get new legal counsel together in the eleventh hour, and we requested a guardian ad litem and custody evaluator to investigate and represent the interests of the kids themselves. After another year of court battles, we won back fifty-fifty custody of my children. The process was grueling, and I was subjected to a competency hearing, among other indignities, but eventually we won, and I was finally able to see my children again.

Despite the fact that at last, I was free, and my life was coming back together in the most immediate and concrete sense, emotional closure and healing would be a long time coming.

TRIAL BY TRIAL

In 2016, seven years after breaking free from Eric, I got a call from a victims' advocate who had worked with me in my domestic violence case against Richard, at which Eric had testified. Given that I was a former victim, she called to let me know that Eric had been arrested and jailed for the assault and rape of two minor girls.

Having lived in fear for all these years that Eric might return, it was a relief knowing that he was finally behind bars. However, that relief was eclipsed by a deep sense of guilt for not pursuing a case against him on my own. I had wanted nothing more than for Eric to permanently disappear from my life, and I felt responsible for what I had, in effect, allowed to happen to these two girls, as well as all the other women he had surely victimized these past few years, because I was too selfish and afraid to go after him. *This should never have happened*, I thought. *I let him off too easy.* This was survivor's guilt, as obviously I wasn't responsible for his reprehensible choices, but I couldn't let go of the guilt.

Six months later, a newspaper article reported on a sting operation in northern Utah that had resulted in the arrest of several human traffickers. No names were listed, but several of the traffickers were from Mexico and another one was from Peru. Barry and I both wondered—*is that Eric?*

Barry called the Department of Homeland Security. While they wouldn't confirm whether Eric was picked up in the sting operation, they did divulge that he was being held by US Immigration and Customs Enforcement and facing a deportation trial.

I told Barry that I had to testify against him. Here was my chance to make right on what I should have done before, what I would have done if I had had the strength and capacity at the time. The court needed to know exactly what he was capable of and what he could do again if he were allowed to stay. I couldn't have that—I wanted him deported.

We contacted the prosecutors. They told us his deportation hearing was almost over. Eric had already given his defense, and the government was presenting its case now. The hearings were almost over already.

"Well, what if we have another witness?" Barry asked over the phone.

They wanted me to write up an overview of the testimony I could provide. We faxed a summary detailing everything Eric had put me through and got it to the prosecutor's desk right before he was set to present closing statements against Eric. They deemed my information important enough to delay the rest of the hearings in order to collect my testimony.

I spent many hours on the phone with the prosecutor, detailing everything that had happened to me. We worked through the details and actually went through receipts, cell phone records, and other evidence to reconstruct every trip Eric had taken me on.

In order to really cinch the case, I needed to testify in person. It would be frightening to come face-to-face with Eric again, but it felt like the only way to get closure and some measure of justice.

I testified against Eric several times, in both a civil case and a stalking injunction, as well as in his deportation trial on behalf of the Department of Homeland Security. Twice, they had Eric video chat from jail, projected up on a big screen in the courtroom, and one time he was there in the flesh. The sight of him twisted my stomach up into knots but seeing him in a prison uniform was a spiritually satisfying experience. Finally, it seemed that there was some justice in the world.

Testifying in front of him was tough, and his team didn't make it any easier on me. They tried to discredit me as a witness by questioning my mental health, and they even brought Richard in to testify about my medical history, never mind that we hadn't been together in seven years. It was incredible to me that Richard had come in to testify, more or less on behalf of Eric, now a known child rapist and human trafficker, simply to get back at me. Thankfully, I didn't have to be present for that. The prosecutor later told me that, while Richard had plenty to say about me, he doubted it would sway the court.

The defense also brought in a nasty letter, supposedly written by my former boss at the preschool, accusing me of being emotionally manipulative and lying about Eric. Given that Teresa had clearly sided with me when Eric was first stalking me, I suspected that the letter had been fabricated.

Regardless of its authenticity, the judge found the letter just as confounding as I did. He did not understand what this woman had to do with the situation at hand or how she could have judged the accuracy of statements made about events at which she wasn't present. Ultimately, the letter probably had little effect on the trial, but it wounded me deeply.

The defense pulled out every dirty trick they could think of. Both Barry and my therapist came to testify on my behalf, but since Eric's attorney claimed he might call them as witnesses, they weren't allowed to hear any prior testimony. As such, they couldn't be present while I testified, although thankfully I had the victims' advocate in the courtroom while facing Eric and his team. They were awful the whole time, heckling me in the courtroom, calling me names, and issuing open threats in the hallway. They were trying to break me down, to make me look hysterical and crazy, anything to discredit me or intimidate me enough that I backed down.

This was terrible, but it didn't work. I had come on a mission, and I wouldn't be scared away. I was tired of being the victim who backed down. I stood before the judge and court and told the whole ugly, evil truth about what he had done to me.

And they knew it was the truth.

Eric had his family there for all three hearings, including the sister who had driven the car on several occasions, shuttling me around for Eric. When I started testifying the first day, she rushed out of the courtroom and threw up right outside in the hallway. We could all hear her from inside the courtroom. She was obviously terrified of what she knew I was about to say, which she could only have known ahead of time *because it was the truth*.

That wasn't just painfully obvious to me, but also to the court, which ultimately moved to have Eric deported. In 2017, Eric was finally removed from the country, sent back to Peru, and barred from ever returning lest he face prosecution for sexual assault of a minor and possibly human trafficking.

I had expected his deportation to make me feel safer, but I began having nightmares about him sneaking back across the border to enact revenge upon me. My brain just could not accept that he was really gone, not yet.

As far as I know, he hasn't come back. We have reason to believe Eric must have informed on other traffickers. Hopefully he is frightened enough of both the law and his former associates to never want to show his face in Utah, or anywhere else in this country, ever again.

Still, you can never be too sure, so I watch my back. We invested in state-of-the-art security systems and took other precautions, for good reason. But I didn't want to live my life in fear. To truly feel safe, I was going to have to do some emotional work to achieve long-term relief from my trauma. Eric could have been dead and buried and I wouldn't have felt entirely free of him.

RUNNING FROM THE PAST

The road through—not just to, but *through*—recovery was grueling. Given my history of cognitive dissonance and denialism, it took me an extremely long time to even *admit* to all my traumas, much less address them effectively.

When I first broke free from Eric, I wouldn't admit to having actually been trafficked, not to Barry or to myself. I kept maintaining that it was just a really toxic relationship. I characterized the trafficking as Eric "sharing" me; I didn't allow myself to think of it in any other way. I just wanted to put it all behind me, having finally extracted myself from both an abusive marriage and another abusive "relationship," as I thought of it. Calling it what it was and actually working through what happened to me? I wasn't interested. I just wanted to move on and be a normal person with a normal life.

For a while, this mindset helped. Barry watched me transform into a whole new person. I felt the freedom to become happier, more confident, and more outgoing—all the traits I had always wanted to have. While not an easy transition for me, as a naturally passive and anxious person, personal growth was much more possible now that I was no longer trapped in toxic environments. I could actually push myself in this domain without having someone's boot on my neck all the time, dragging me down and tearing me apart.

As significant as my personality transformation appeared on the outside, it was always shaky under the surface. There were good days and bad ones, and it was hard to maintain. The coping methods I was using to keep me stable weren't necessarily healthy, even if they appeared so on the surface. I was no longer cutting or inflicting any conventional self-harm, but I was over-exercising. I would ride my bike sixty to seventy miles and then go hiking with weights strapped around my ankles, only to get up and do it all again the next morning.

I needed to wear myself out daily just to put on the veneer of a calm, well-adjusted wife and mom for Barry and the kids to come home to at the end of the day. I literally couldn't stand still, or my anxiety would start to escalate. Being alone with my thoughts was too depressing, so I never allowed myself time to sit with them. I was literally trying to outrun my past. I could feel it behind me, like a tsunami, lapping at my heels, and if I stopped—I would drown. So I simply never stopped moving.

I was still in therapy, even opening up more than before, but not by much. I couldn't come to grips with the fact that I had been abused. Richard was my shitty ex-husband, not my abuser.

Eric was a sick man who had "shared me" with others, and that was all. As for what happened with my dad during my childhood, I had suppressed the memories entirely. There was no telling the truth to my therapist when I couldn't even admit it to myself. I just kept lying and running, running and lying.

You can't outrun the past, though, not forever. All these traumas were still with me, and my ability to keep them suppressed began to falter after four or five years of going on this way.

A turning point came for me when I decided to take a big step with Barry. I was sitting next to him on the plane on the way back from a trip to Phoenix, feeling very close, and I picked up my phone to text him even though he was sitting right there, shoulder to shoulder with me.

Do you want to have a baby with me?

Barry looked down at his phone and then over at me as if I were crazy. He thought us too old for a baby, our lives too hectic, as we already had five children in various stages of life between the two of us. I kept pushing the matter, though, and eventually he conceded, but only if we adopted. I don't think he thought they would let us adopt at our age, but we put in the paperwork and six months later we had our little baby girl.

Being the mother of an infant again forced me to slow down since I could no longer spend every waking minute out running myself ragged. I had to be home to take care of the baby, which meant I now had more time to sit with my thoughts. Suppressed memories started bubbling to the surface, and they became harder and harder to force back down.

This push and pull made me feel so physically unwell that my doctor thought I had colon cancer at first. My symptoms were that bad. But all my tests came back negative. So they ran more tests to figure out what was wrong with me. I spent a year getting pricked, poked, and prodded for lab work and exams. Cancer? No. Multiple sclerosis? No. Autoimmune disorder? Nope. They tested me for every chronic and degenerative disease imaginable, but I always came back with a clean bill of health. My lab work was always normal.

But I didn't *feel* normal; I didn't feel okay. Things got so bad that I was spending more and more time just lying in bed, unable to really move. This went on so long we had to get a nanny for the baby since I was so useless and Barry was still running all his businesses. My body seemed to be betraying me, and I worried that I was actually dying, no matter what the tests had to say about it.

Before long, it became clear that my mental health was the problem and I was going to need professional help again—not just a therapist, but much more.

Barry agreed and took the matter seriously. We toured various therapy clinics and other facilities throughout Utah, but none of them seemed like the right fit. Many resembled the psychiatric hospitals I had stayed at before, which were hellish and only made things worse. Those hospitals focused on addiction and mental disorders rooted in pharmacological imbalances. What I needed was a team that understood how to treat trauma, but we didn't really understand this at the time.

Barry could not possibly have understood this because I was still in denial myself about the exact nature of what I had been subjected to.

DRASTIC MEASURES

Barry was listening to the radio one day and heard an ad from a new treatment center promoting their groundbreaking treatments for anxiety and depression. We hadn't considered alternative therapies, but having tried everything else, we thought, *why not give it a go?* I had nothing to lose at this point. Nothing else was working.

The program was expensive, as treatment centers tend to be, but they offered radical alternative therapies in addition to conventional talk therapy. They had this contraption, which I nicknamed "the spinning coffin," that looked like a tanning bed on a merry-go-round. They would hook me up to electrodes and play music over headphones while spinning me in circles for a half hour at a time. This was extremely disorienting and made me dizzy and nauseated. I would stagger to the recovery room, holding on to the walls to keep myself up straight.

The therapist wanted to serve me shakes that he claimed would help my brain recover. This triggered memories of Eric and Richard drugging me, so I refused to drink them. This might seem paranoid, just an artifact of my abuse, but the therapist made me uncomfortable. During a therapy session, he once started talking about his wife and girlfriends and his own sexual desires, which was totally inappropriate. When they asked me to lie naked in another medical bed that didn't spin but simply latched closed and bathed you in bright light, I had the eerie sensation of being watched.

None of this sat right with me, and after about seven days of this kind of thing, I had had enough. I marched right out the front door and hiked up the canyon to a nearby ski resort. I called Barry and told him I wasn't going back.

Later that night, I looked up the therapist online and found him on the sex offenders registry. I was horrified that this sexual predator was running a program for vulnerable women, pressing them to strip down under the guise of strange experiments and talking to them about inappropriate topics in therapy.

Barry went to the facility the next day to demand our money back, letting them know he was aware of the therapist's past. The facility eventually refunded our money, but the whole experience was demoralizing and obviously ineffective.

Expanding our search to include treatment centers outside of Utah, we looked at several in California. One facility was literally a dump in the middle of the woods, complete with bugs crawling everywhere. The cottages in which they housed patients had big glass windows that would have made me feel unnaturally exposed. Other centers had long waitlists that were impractical—I needed immediate help.

It quickly became clear California wasn't going to work, either, so we started looking farther afield, out in Tennessee, where we found an inpatient facility called Brookhaven with various modalities of therapy, such as equine therapy. The fee was exorbitant, albeit in the same range as other centers. All things considered, Brookhaven made a good impression, so Barry wrote a check for $150,000 on the spot. I had the next thirty days to work through my trauma.

We spent most of our time doing arts and crafts. They offered group therapy and very few one-on-one sessions, which made it impossible for me to disclose anything meaningful. I was reticent about my past as it was. The whole thing felt like a big waste of money, so I called Barry and told him to get me out of there. He took the first flight down to come get me, but the staff didn't want to let me out of the program. They threatened to call the cops on me if we left, since I was under their care now. They made us jump through a bunch of hoops before finally letting me out of the contract.

We got a hotel room in downtown Knoxville and holed up there for several days. The medical staff at Brookhaven had put me on a powerful medication called Klonopin but refused to give me a prescription to wean myself off, likely to get back at me for leaving early. This meant that I had to go off the Klonopin cold turkey, which sent me into hellish withdrawals for several days. My whole body was shaking, and the rebound anxiety made me feel like I wanted to throw myself out the window. Barry had to hold me down just to keep me safe.

I started to feel better after a few days, but we decided to stay and look for other treatment options in Knoxville since we were already there. I didn't want to go back to Utah. Brookhaven had been a bad fit for me but being in Tennessee was good for my recovery. It would be easier to heal here, far away from everything that had happened to me back out West.

We looked for local therapists and found a woman running an intensive outpatient program called Fairhaven. She was actually a former employee from Brookhaven and was trained in the various modalities they employed, but her program promised a more intimate experience. The promise of intimacy was certainly accurate, although the treatment was not as effective as I had hoped.

Patients were allowed to go home on nights and weekends but spent five days a week in treatment. The director was pleasant over the phone and in person, and confident in her ability to help, so I decided to give it a shot even though my expectations were low at this point. I enrolled and started looking for an apartment in Knoxville.

They gave me an intake form to fill out at home. Barry was reading and watching television while I sat there answering a series of questions about my past. They wanted to know about my childhood and my relationship with my parents. Answering these questions started to make me feel upset when I suddenly had the epiphany that my responses were lies. This wasn't my childhood—it was fiction. The same fiction I had been telling therapists for years.

Anxious and starting to hyperventilate, I had to excuse myself to the bathroom to calm down. I ran the water in the bath and lay in it. Something was rising up in me, memories of the past, and I was hit with a sudden realization, a surfacing of suppressed truths.

I cried out for Barry, who came rushing in.

"Hold my hands!" I cried, needing his touch, his hands on mine to keep me from clawing out my own eyeballs.

He took my hands and asked what was going on.

"My dad abused me as a kid," I said, letting the words hang there. He understood what I meant.

This revelation opened up a whole new array of traumas that I needed to confront in order to heal. Domestic violence, trafficking, and now child abuse—this horrible trifecta of abuse had put me in this terrible state.

When we went to see the new therapist the next morning and hand in the form, this time, at long last, revealing the entire truth of *why* I felt this way, she was unsurprised.

"I suspected, to be honest," she said, adding that it made no difference in her ability to help me overcome my trauma. She told me this was quite common among trafficking victims, as most sex workers were abused as children. Predators prey on the damaged, which was probably why so many of them had targeted me throughout my life.

Barry returned to Utah, as he had to get back to his job. I stayed in Knoxville for just over a year, working with this woman and her partner. The two of them became good friends, *too* good of friends, in fact; their relationship with me crossed a number of professional boundaries that should never have been crossed. We began spending time together socially on nights and weekends, talking and texting on the phone all the time, going out for dinner and concerts and more. We were always together, even when I wasn't in treatment.

Her theory, as she put it, was that integrating herself so thoroughly into my life made it easier for her to help me heal. That made sense to me at first, and I welcomed the company, but things started to get weird. For instance, they were buying a house and wanted me to move in with them. They invited me along to a showing to pick out "my" room.

Of course, I was only in Knoxville for therapy and would eventually return home to Barry and the kids. Not coincidentally, their opinion of him had soured. They tried to convince me he was having an affair by making a big deal out of an innocuous text he had sent a potential babysitter. Barry had put a smiley face at the end of the text, and it was my therapists' opinion that no one would do this unless they were having an affair.

Barry and I actually ended up separating for six weeks under their suggestion, completely ceasing communication, since they thought I needed distance from the relationship. They felt that I needed to let myself grow and explore because I had missed out on being an unattached young single woman due to my father's abuse and then my early marriage. When we worked out together at the gym, they pushed me to go out with guys who were hitting on us. This felt wrong, but here were the therapists who were supposed to make me better telling me that this is what I *needed* to do to get better.

They clearly wanted Barry and me to split up, which made me increasingly uncomfortable. I decided to leave the program. I was supposed to be getting better and becoming more independent, but I had instead grown strangely dependent upon them. Though I knew I should just return home, they convinced me to first come along on a Florida retreat, promising me that we would work out a new path forward for my recovery upon our return.

They had me drive separately in my own car all the way from Tennessee down to Florida and didn't stay with me on the highway as they'd promised. I got lost somewhere in Georgia with no cell signal. It was horrible. I ended up calling Barry so he could help me figure out my location by map. By the time I got back on track and arrived in Florida, I was stressed out and in tears, feeling like a complete idiot for ever agreeing to come along.

When I called my therapists to meet up, they said they weren't free until the next day. Tomorrow came, and they kept putting me off—first one hour, then another hour, then another. By the time I finally met up with them at the retreat, I had had it with the whole thing.

"You know what, I don't think you guys give a damn about me," I said. "You're just stringing me along and robbing us blind."

We had paid an insane amount of money for more than a year of treatment, and in addition to my lack of recovery, the codependency they had encouraged had only exacerbated my stress.

I decided to cut ties right then and there and drove back to Tennessee alone. Barry was waiting at my apartment, having flown in on an emergency flight. Another year had passed, and I still felt that I was right back at square one.

THE RECOVERY PROCESS

In fact, I actually had made some crucial progress over my year-long stint. Specifically, at long last, I was able to fully acknowledge what all had happened to me as a child. In addition, Fairhaven gave me the language to understand what Eric had done to me. Eric wasn't "sharing" me with others: he was a human trafficker, and I was being trafficked for sex. Simply owning what happened was a major step toward managing my trauma. I was finally able to tell Barry exactly what I had suffered. Although this was difficult for him to hear, we were finally able to work through things with a mutual understanding of the truth.

My psychiatrist wanted me to file a formal complaint against my therapists for crossing inappropriate boundaries, but it was more important for me to focus on my own healing. She helped me find another hospital, a more traditional facility, to start working with instead. They had a long waitlist, but after a short phone consultation, they invited me down and accepted me into the inpatient facility. The program was only two weeks, and while it too was expensive, these were real professionals. They did lab work, which again came back clean, and diagnosed me with a psychosomatic condition. This didn't mean the physical distress I was experiencing wasn't real, they explained, just that I was suffering from a complex post-traumatic stress disorder induced by trauma, and that I wasn't going to get better until I worked through that trauma.

They were able to arrange a consultation for me with a well-known psychiatrist, Dr. James A. Chu, who is basically a rock star in the psychology world in terms of trauma treatment. His book, *Rebuilding Shattered Lives*, resonated with me more than anything I had ever read in my life. It felt like he was describing my life—my history, my personality type, my problems, everything about me. Finally, here was someone who really understood what I was going through and not just empathized with me but understood what was wrong.

Dr. Chu set me up with a new team of providers and therapists who actually seemed interested in helping me get better, not just draining our bank accounts. I worked with them on an outpatient basis, and it was clear that with this team behind me, I was finally going to get better.

It wasn't easy, though. In fact, recovery has been the hardest thing I have ever experienced. Recovery from trauma has been harder than surviving the abuse itself. When I was being abused, my brain simply shut off. In recovery, I had to dig down into myself and face what had happened to me, with both eyes open.

Recovery is an active process. They call it the recovery *process* for a reason. Surviving horrific abuse is simple...not easy...but simple. You do what you have to do to survive. That meant letting my handlers shuffle me around until I could get away. But in recovery, there were more complex choices to be made. How would I handle my trauma? Who would I tell and what would

I tell them and when and how? If I was going to get better, I had to take an active role in my recovery. Dissociating, compartmentalizing, cutting—these were not the answers. Facing the brutal truth was the answer.

And it *was* brutal. Recovery sometimes made the urge to kill myself even more intense than the suicidal feelings I had experienced during the abuse.

The process still isn't over. Years later, I am still in therapy almost every day. I will probably be in therapy, and in recovery, for the rest of my life, and that's okay. I am still getting better, still discovering myself, still reclaiming a sense of purpose in life.

Purpose and healing are related. My whole life, all my suffering had seemed utterly senseless. There was no purpose to any of it, in effect making my life seem as pointless as the abuse itself. When I faced my trauma head-on and started to overcome it, I became motivated to help others do the same. That's my purpose for being *now*, but I had to heal and find myself first before I could be an advocate for others.

No one should have to go through what I suffered. I want to keep people from making the same mistakes I did. I also want communities to improve at recognizing trafficking and abuse. I want people to be able to identify potential victims, the way I spotted Bella—whether they know a Bella or they *are* a Bella.

To that end, my goal in writing this book is to use my experience to help others recognize what is happening to them, put words to their experiences, and see that they too can come out on the other side.

Trauma keeps us from living life and developing into the person we want to be, even after the abuse stops. You actually *can* pursue a healthy relationship, a family, different hobbies or careers, or a community in a way that trauma makes seem impossible. But first you need to face your trauma. You can't run and hide forever. My story should be instructive—trauma always catches up, no matter how fast you run.

My traumas were severe, but they are hardly exceptional. Millions of people worldwide are being trafficked at any moment, and far more are facing domestic abuse right now. Those who get out alive may be able to hide from their trauma for a time, as I did, but eventually the past catches up with you. There's no way around or past your trauma. The only way out is through.

Most people won't be able to navigate the recovery process alone. You need therapists and other providers, good ones who understand trauma and its treatment. Opening up to them will not be easy, nor will opening up to yourself and digging down into your own pain. In fact, it might feel like it will kill you, but I promise it won't. What kills people is running from their trauma and bottling it up inside. Dealing with trauma only *feels* like it will kill you. In truth, you're actually learning how to live.

Abuse will change who you are for the rest of your life—that is true—but it doesn't have to define who you are. There is life after abuse, life after trafficking, life after trauma. And it can be a beautiful life, even if it's still hard. My life isn't perfect now. I take the bad days with the good. But life is sweeter now than ever before, with none of it taken for granted. Having lost my children for the better part of a year and having barely been around for the first five years of my younger daughter's life because I was in treatment, I now cherish each day with them, so much more than before. Everything tastes sweeter when you come out the other side a survivor, but only if you get the help you need to overcome trauma.

The shame and self-loathing you feel doesn't belong to you. That shame belongs to your trafficker, to your abuser, not to you. You aren't awful because someone did awful things to you. The only thing it says about you is that you were strong enough to survive.

You survived abuse. You can survive trauma as well. Even though things may feel hard now, the reins are back in your hands. Choice can feel oppressive when you have lived without free will for so long, but once you are free you can actually put in the work to get better. You are free to work on yourself, have faith, believe in yourself, believe in others, accept help and kindness, and face the pain that's been keeping you from living.

You didn't die. I promise you, you can live.

TRAFFICKING INFORMATION

My story may be dramatic and the specifics unique to me—but too many other trafficking victims have similar tales. Although the general public tends to think of slavery, even sex slavery, as a practice of another time, trafficking is an all-too-common occurrence in the modern world. This is particularly true of sex trafficking, which is the most prevalent form of human trafficking and slavery in the modern world.

The full scope of the problem is difficult to quantify. Trafficked people are, by their very nature, an invisible population. They are disappeared and secreted away, ferried from location to location—out of sight and out of mind of the public. We are taken from our families and communities, isolated, and kept unseen. Most victims are never identified, never interact with the outside world, and never get to tell their story to anyone who might be able to help.

In 2020, the National Human Trafficking Hotline received over fifty thousand substantive tips and reports of human trafficking. Most of these dealt with sex trafficking, as do most domestic cases of trafficking within the United States. According to data from the Federal Bureau of Investigation, collected under its Uniform Crime Reporting Program, most reported and prosecuted trafficking cases in the United States fall under the category of "commercial sex acts." According to the Polaris Project, a nonprofit nongovernmental organization working to combat and prevent sex and labor trafficking in North America, there were over ten thousand trafficking situations identified in 2020 with just over sixteen thousand identified victims. About two-thirds of these were sex trafficking victims—10,836, to be precise.

These known cases are only the tip of the iceberg, however. Best estimates suggest that fewer than one in two hundred survivors of sex trafficking are ever identified. On any given day, there are approximately forty million people across the globe working in forced labor, often under the guise of arranged marriage, according to *Global Estimates of Modern Slavery*, a report published by Alliance 8.7 and other partnership organizations, including the U.S. Department of Labor. Many of these are victims of sex trafficking, including the kind of commercialized sexual exploitation that I was forced into.

While trafficking touches all kinds of people, this kind of commercial sexual exploitation is a problem primarily facing women. According to data from the Counter Trafficking Data

Collaborative (CTDC), a project begun in 2017 to collect and harmonize data being put out by various counter-trafficking organizations around the globe, just over half of all trafficking victims in the world currently reside in North America, and while 84 percent of them are women, another 15 percent are male, with the remaining 1 percent mostly trans women. However, when looking specifically at commercialized sex work, over 99 percent of sex trafficking victims are women (though given the scope of the problem, this still means thousands upon thousands of victims are young boys, and their stories should be neither ignored nor forgotten). More than a third of these victims are children under the age of eighteen, and 10 percent of those are children under the age of nine. These are our women, our girls, our boys—and they are being victimized all across the country.

In the United States, Nevada has the highest rate of human trafficking, with 7.38 individuals out of 100,000 being trafficked at any given moment (according to the 2020 *National Human Trafficking Hotline Data Report*), which is largely the consequence of the state's notorious sex industry, but the problem pervades the entire nation. Even the smallest states and wealthiest counties see significant rates of human trafficking. Utah, where I was first trafficked, ranks somewhere in the middle. It can happen anywhere. No place is totally safe.

While the U.S. Department of Justice issued a 2021 report, *Human Trafficking Data Collection Activities*, indicating that nine out of ten defendants prosecuted for human trafficking in U.S. districts are eventually convicted, the vast majority of traffickers are never brought to justice because their crimes and victims are never identified. Every day, millions of trafficked victims go about their horrific lives unseen.

Ending the scourge of trafficking will involve bringing victims and their stories to light. They will never be found if we don't acknowledge their plight. We need to know about them and what they face. We need to understand that trafficking exists and how it looks in the modern world. We can only find victims by looking for them. We have to know *where* to look and *what* we are looking for.

Frequently, trafficking is a very "personal" crime in that victims are often trafficked by people they know, including family members and intimate partners. According to 2020 data from the Polaris Project, about one in three traffickers are known to their victims before the crime takes place. As many as one in five are intimate partners. However, these statistics are murky since these situations are murky. In my case, I wasn't actually in a sexual relationship with my trafficker, though I convinced myself that I was after he raped me for the first time.

In truth, traffickers almost always know what they are doing, and they systematically seek out victims. In 2020, amid the COVID-19 lockdowns, the internet became the top location where traffickers found their victims, with reports of trafficking on popular social media sites doubling within a single year, according to the Polaris Project. Whether they are looking online, in bars, at the workplace, or inside the home, traffickers are constantly seeking out their victims.

Wherever traffickers first find their victims, trafficking often looks the same. I wrote this book to help people understand the signs. By telling my story, I hope to give a voice to other victims as well, the ones nobody hears from. All victims have their own personal story to tell—it's just, in the ways that matter most, the same horrific story, again and again.

By stepping out of the darkness and speaking up, I hope to bring them into the light as well. They are all around us, if we could only see and hear them.

CPSIA information can be obtained
at www.ICGtesting.com
Printed in the USA
BVHW071936130423
662312BV00003B/57

9 781544 540337